NEW DIRECTIONS
IN THE THEORY AND RESEARCH OF
SERIOUS LEISURE

NEW DIRECTIONS
IN THE THEORY AND RESEARCH OF
SERIOUS LEISURE

Robert A. Stebbins

The Edwin Mellen Press
Lewiston•Queenston•Lampeter

Library of Congress Cataloging-in-Publication Data

Stebbins, Robert A., 1938-
   New directions in the theory and research of serious leisure / Robert A. Stebbins.
     p. cm. --
   Includes bibliographical references (p.) and index.
   ISBN 0-7734-7601-6
   1. Leisure--Social aspects. I. Title.

GV14.45 .S84 2001
306.4'812--dc21

                          00-060934

hors série.

A CIP catalog record for this book is available from the British Library.

Copyright © 2001 Robert A. Stebbins

The Edwin Mellen Press
Box 450
Lewiston, New York
USA 14092-0450

The Edwin Mellen Press
Box 67
Queenston, Ontario
CANADA L0S 1L0

The Edwin Mellen Press, Ltd.
Lampeter, Ceredigion, Wales
UNITED KINGDOM SA48 8LT

Printed in the United States of America

To Gus and Terry Brannigan

Table of Contents

Preface

Where do we find solidarity in advanced capitalist societies? The chief normative sources devised under industrialization are all in crisis. The nuclear family persists, but high divorce rates and the increasing geographical and social mobility of children, weaken its influence. Secularization has contributed to the deinstitutionalization and deregulation of the Church. The continued popularity of astrology and spiritualism, together with the explosion of New Age cults in the last quarter of the twentieth century, suggest that the desire for spiritual belonging and recognition is widespread. But compared with the high water mark of ecumenicalism in the nineteenth century, it is diffuse and unstable. Globalization has eroded the primacy of the nation-state, and multi-culturalism has recast the politics of national identity. The traditional political parties of right and left seem unable to engage meaningfully with the diversity of multi-cultural values and lifestyles. The meaning of Body and Nature, which used to be unequivocal foundations of solidarity, are revised by the replacement technologies and genetic engineering of science. Even work, the last redoubt of solidarity in the heroic age of industrialization, is no longer the rock of character or community. The rise of the service sector in Western society in the 1980s produced massive delayering throughout manufacturing, and the transference of many production functions from the core to the periphery. The traditional idea of a job for life disappeared in the process. Labour today lives with higher levels of uncertainty than at any time since the last world war.

Modernity is conventionally understood to be a social and economic formation which incorporates ceaseless change as a feature of the system. But the transformation in Western society during the last thirty years seem more far reaching and turbulent than anything in recent history. Economic restructuring and the attrition of the welfare state suggest a return to the Hobbesian war of all against all. Of course, Hobbes's solution to this natural state of anarchy, namely the social contract, which recognizes individual rights and civil responsibilities, is still a cornerstone of citizenship. But the destruction of traditional communities as capital flees from primary and secondary sectors, to the less labour intensive knowledge and service sectors, demonstrates the elasticity of the citizenship net. The pursuit of competitive advantage in the global market has ripped holes in this net which are terrifyingly wide.

Appropriate then that leisure, which Emile Durkheim, writing on the new, emerging moral individualism of his own day over one hundred years ago, described as 'the less serious' side of life, has become so serious as a source of meaning and solidarity today. In this, rich and penetrating book, Robert Stebbins, who coined the term 'serious leisure' nearly 20 years ago, provides the best moral and sociological analysis of the phenomenon. He shows that serious leisure is now the staple for many forms of social solidarity and identity cohesion. Whereas Durkheim looked to the reformed Church, the State and organized groups of labour, to produce collective moral remaking, Stebbins demonstrates that volunteering, participation in knowledge and arts cultures and cultural tourism actually produce deeper and more binding meaning and solidarity today. Meaning and solidarity are practically made through the direct act of sensual and rational engagement between the self, the Natural world and society.

One of the great virtues of the book is that it underscores the creative capacities of humans to develop stable, meaningful agendas of voluntary activities that have demonstrable psychic and social benefits. The volunteers and hobbyist's studied by Stebbins are clearly having fun, but they do not treat fun as an end in itself, but rather as a means of moral remaking. It is a refreshing set of insights to bring to leisure theory. Most discussion on the main trends of leisure in everyday life under advanced capitalism focuses on negatives: the increasing velocity of life which creates a time-famine for pleasurable and improving activities; the differentiation and dislocation of relations which contributes to the sense of isolation and episodic structure in everyday life; the turn towards alcohol and drug dependency as a means of neutralizing feelings of invalidation; and the perceived amorality of many forms of pleasure taking, in the form of pornography, violence and other types of transgressive conduct. It is a sorry roll-call, and were one to read it consistently one would have to conclude that leisure has been stripped of its canonical status as that sphere of life in which opportunities for freedom, choice and pleasure are concentrated.

Stebbins touches upon some of these trends in his discussion of causal leisure. But he stops well short of turning leisure activities into the portmanteaux of a general theory of alienation. Rather, what emerges powerfully from the discussion is that human beings, just as Thomas Hobbes and later Segment Freud argued, are essentially learning animals. The individual pursuit of gratification produces censure if it ignores tolerance and respect for others. Through this censure, mankind has fashioned an ideal of civilization and standards of self restraint. We may regularly fall short of both the ideal and standards in our leisure and associated behavior. But we have the capacity to learn from our experience and to pass on learning to others. This is one of the great civic virtues of serious leisure. It is a way of making and communicating meaning which enhances solidarity through non-directive and non-judgmental participation. The moral remaking of collective life emerges through the trial and error of participating in structured activity. It is one of the best expressions of citizenship.

Bob Stebbins is an unusual theorist of leisure. Not only does he expertly decipher the important trends of the day, he practices with aplomb, serious leisure. Anyone who spends time in his company at a conference or social event is aware of being in the presence of an acute mind and a generous spirit. More than that, anyone

Who travels to that Shangri-La of the Southern states, New Orleans, will find that Bob's travel guide to the city is the tourist's bible. This is indeed, how serious leisure should be, engaging, affirming and enlarging.

Serious Leisure will be devoured by students and specialists in Leisure Studies and the sociology of leisure. It is the culmination of nearly two decades work on the subject, and it will be quickly recognized as the benchmark work in the field. The practice of serious leisure extends conventional concepts of citizenship and solidarity, at a time in which the central normative institutions of social order are perceived as being in a state of crisis. This book is a route-map to the moral, psychological and sociological significance of serious leisure. Those who refuse to follow it, ignore one of the unique characteristics which helps us to elucidate the true meaning of our times.

Chris Rojek
Professor of Sociology & Culture
Theory, Culture & Society Center
Nottingham Tent University

Foreword

The term "serious leisure" first appeared in print in 1982, a neologism that I authored to identify and summarily describe its three types: the activities of amateurs, hobbyists, and career volunteers. I did not invent the types, nor was I the first to write about them; long before I came to leisure studies many a philosopher and social scientist had discussed one or more of them from a variety of angles. Rather, my contribution since 1973, when I first began research in this area, has been to systematically explore a reasonably large sample of amateur, hobbyist, and career volunteer activities, to combine these studies into an ever more elaborate grounded theory of serious leisure, and to extend the theory into certain areas of social life on which its unique perspective could shed some useful new light.

At first I was alone in this endeavor, although not for long. By the mid-1980s, my first book in the area - *Amateurs: On the margin between work and leisure* (published in 1979) - had stimulated a handful of researchers to study the leisure of amateurs. Their empirical and theoretical efforts were integrated along with my own in *Amateurs, professionals, and serious leisure* (published in 1992), the writing of which was completed by 1991. But a significantly larger amount of work on serious leisure has been completed since 1991, and so the time has come to take stock once again. The present book, then, is just such a stock taking; it encompasses not only all the works written under the banner of serious leisure since the benchmark year of 1991, but also some that had been written before that date, research and theory I somehow overlooked while preparing the 1992 book.

And a great deal has been written. Part I contains the basic perspective of serious leisure as it stands in early 1999, starting with chapter 1 where I present four major conceptual additions - lifestyle, social world, leisure identity, and central life interest - along with a statement about the five levels of analysis, all these ideas having been only alluded to in the 1992 statement. Two lengthier additions appear as chapters 2 and 3 on the liberal arts hobbies and career volunteering, while chapter 4 on casual leisure presents the clearest and most detailed treatment yet of the boundaries separating it from serious leisure. My intent in all this is to present enough of the basic perspective to enable this book to stand on its own, forcing the reader to go to its 1992 predecessor only for certain details.

In addition, the present book contains some of my far-flung articles and chapters on serious leisure, thereby giving readers easier access to them than heretofore while allowing them to be integrated into the basic perspective. These are reprinted in Parts I, II, and IV (chapters 2 through 6 and 10), where they have gone through considerable updating and excision of repetitious sections. Part II contains four extensions of the perspective into tourism (chapter 5), selfishness (chapter 6), and adult education and disability treated under the heading of leisure education (chapter 7). Chapter 8 of Part III revolves around recent theory and research in the field of serious leisure, where the intent is to show how far we have come along the road leading to a mature field. The next chapter centers on various theoretical issues that have arisen over the years, none of which is resolved, however, although I hope I have moved us in significant measure toward resolution. Serious leisure in the twenty-first century is the subject of Part IV. Here, in chapter 10, I examine its role in the modern age of domination by electronic technology, where on the average, more and more people are spending less and less time at work when compared with the past. In chapter 11, the Conclusion, we consider several new directions for theory and research as well as take a look at a couple of new fields ripe for the application of serious leisure theory: leisure education and community development.

To this point in time, most of the empirical support for the theory presented in this book has come from my own qualitative/exploratory research on amateurs, hobbyists, and career volunteers. To avoid repeated author-date citations to this literature, I will, where appropriate, simply refer globally to my past research and leave it at that. That research includes, amateurs in classical music, theater, archaeology, astronomy, baseball and Canadian football, and stand-up comedy and entertainment magic. These eight studies made up the fifteen-year long "project" on which much of the 1992 book was based. Subsequently, I examined the hobby of barbershop singing as well as a couple of the liberal arts hobbies, notably language acquisition and cultural tourism. Finally, in 1997, I completed an exploration of career volunteers in the francophone subcommunities of Calgary and Edmonton in Canada. All these studies are either listed in the Bibliography of this book or reprinted and updated as one of its chapters. This having been said, a reading of the following pages will reveal that other researchers have also contributed considerable empirical support to the perspective and are doing so at an increasing rate.

Let us turn to the basic perspective of serious leisure and its recent additions.

Part I The Basic Perspective

Chapter 1

Serious Leisure: An Overview

The term "serious leisure" made its debut in leisure studies circles in 1982. The initial statement (Stebbins, 1982) and several more recent ones centered on the nature of serious leisure, which is now reasonably well expressed in what seems to have become the standard abbreviated definition of this type of activity: Serious leisure is the systematic pursuit of an amateur, hobbyist, or volunteer activity that participants find so substantial and interesting that, in the typical case, they launch themselves on a career centered on acquiring and expressing its special skills, knowledge, and experience (Stebbins, 1992, p. 3). Because of the widespread tendency to see the idea of career as applying only to occupations, note that, in this definition, I use the term much more broadly, following Goffman's (1961, pp. 127-128) elaboration of the idea of "moral career." Broadly conceived, careers are available in all substantial, complicated roles, including especially those in work, leisure, deviance, politics, religion, and interpersonal relationships (see also, Lindesmith, Strauss, and Denzin, 1991, p. 277; Hewitt, 1991, p. 246). As for the definition just presented, it is probably as good a depiction of this form of leisure as can be presented in a one-sentence definition.

I hope it is clear that the adjective "serious" (a word my respondents often used) embodies such qualities as earnestness, sincerity, importance, and carefulness, rather than gravity, solemnity, joylessness, distress, and anxiety. Although the second set of terms occasionally describe serious leisure events, they are uncharacteristic of them and fail to nullify, or, in many cases, even dilute, the overall satisfaction gained by the participants.

To sharpen our understanding of it, serious leisure is commonly contrasted with "casual" or "unserious" leisure, the immediately intrinsically rewarding, relatively short-lived pleasurable activity requiring little or no special training to enjoy it (Stebbins, 1997a). Its types, which will be discussed in detail in chapter 4, include play (including dabbling), relaxation (e.g., sitting, napping, strolling), passive entertainment (e.g., TV, books, recorded music), active entertainment (e.g., games of chance, party games), sociable conversation, and sensory stimulation (e.g., sex, eating, drinking). It is considerably less substantial and offers no career of the sort just described for serious leisure. Casual leisure can also be defined residually as all leisure not classifiable as amateur, hobbyist, or career volunteering.

The Nature of Serious Leisure

To gain a more complete understanding of serious leisure, we must move beyond the handy but nonetheless limited one-sentence definition to look more closely at its three basic types. Amateurs are found in art, science, sport, and entertainment, where they are inevitably linked in several ways with their professional counterparts. For their part, the professionals are identified and defined according to theory developed in the social scientific study of the professions, a substantially more exact procedure than the ones relying on the simplistic and not infrequently commercially-shaped commonsense images of these workers. In other words, when studying amateurs and professionals descriptive definitions turn out to be too superficial, such as observing that the activity in question constitutes a livelihood for the second but not the first or that the second works full-time at it whereas the first pursues it part-time. Rather, we learn much more by noting, for example, that the two are locked in and therefore defined by a system of relations linking professionals, amateurs, and their publics ("the P-A-P system") that has far greater complexity than can be described here (discussed in more detail in Stebbins, 1979, 1992, chap. 3).

Hobbyists lack this professional alter ego, even if they sometimes have commercial equivalents and often have small publics who take an interest in what they do. Hobbyists can be classified according to one of five categories: collectors, makers and tinkerers, activity participants (in noncompetitive, rule-based, pursuits), players of sports and games (where no professional counterparts exist), and enthusiasts in one of the liberal arts. Fishing (Yoder, 1997), bushwalking (Hamilton-Smith, 1993), and barbershop singing (Stebbins, 1996a) exemplify the third, while curling (Apostle, 1992), long-distance running (Yair, 1990), and competitive swimming (Hastings, Kurth, Schloder, & Cyr, 1995) exemplify the fourth. Liberal arts hobbyists are enamored of the systematic acquisition of knowledge for its own sake. This is typically accomplished by reading voraciously in a field of art, sport, cuisine, language, culture, history, science, philosophy, politics, or literature The initial definition and description of the liberal arts hobbies (Stebbins, 1994a), because it is a recent addition to the basic framework, is reprinted and updated as chapter 2 of this book.

Volunteers, the third basic type, engage in volunteering, defined and described by Jon Van Til (1988, p. 6) as follows:

> *Volunteering* may be identified as a helping action of an individual that is valued by him or her, and yet is not aimed directly at material gain or mandated or coerced by others. Thus, in the broadest sense, *volunteering* is an uncoerced helping activity that is engaged in not primarily for financial gain and not by coercion or mandate. It is thereby different in definition from work, slavery, or conscription.

It should be noted, however, that the field of career volunteering is narrower, even if it does cover considerable ground. The taxonomy published in *After work* (Stebbins, 1998a, pp. 74-80), which consists of 16 types of organizational volunteering, shows the scope of career volunteering. Career volunteers provide a great variety of services in education, science, civic affairs (advocacy projects, professional and labor organizations), spiritual development, health, economic development, religion, politics, government (programs and services), human relationships, recreation, and the arts. Some of these volunteers work in the fields of safety or the physical environment, while others prefer to provide necessities (e.g., food, clothing, shelter) or support services. Although much of career volunteering appears to be connected in some way with an organization of some sort, the scope of this leisure is possibly even broader, perhaps including the kinds of helping devoted individuals do for social movements or for neighbors and family.[1] Still, the definition of serious leisure restricts attention everywhere to volunteering in which the participant can find a career, in which there is more or less continuous and substantial helping, rather than one-time donations of money, organs, services, and the like (Stebbins, 1996b). Because the first statement of career volunteering has been considerably expanded and reworked since 1991, the journal article reporting these changes (Stebbins, 1996b) is reprinted, with updated material, as chapter 3.

Serious leisure is further defined by six distinctive qualities, which are found among amateurs, hobbyists, and volunteers alike. One is the occasional need to *persevere*, as seen in confronting danger (e.g., in eating wild mushrooms and climbing mountains, Fine & Holyfield, 1996), managing stage fright (e.g., when participating in theater and sport, Stebbins, 1981) or handling embarrassment (e.g., while doing volunteer work, Floro, 1978, p. 198). Yet, it is clear that positive feelings about the activity come, to some extent, from sticking with it through thick and thin, from conquering adversity. A second quality is, as indicated earlier, that of finding a *career* in the endeavor, shaped as it is by its own special contingencies, turning points and stages of achievement or involvement.

Most, if not all, careers in serious leisure owe their existence to its third quality: serious leisure participants make a significant personal *effort* based on specially acquired *knowledge*, *training*, or *skill*, and, indeed at times, all three. Examples include such achievements as showmanship, athletic prowess, scientific knowledge, and long experience in a role. Fourth, a number of *durable benefits*, or *outcomes*, of serious leisure have so far been identified, mostly from research on amateurs and hobbyists. They include self-actualization, self-enrichment, self-expression, regeneration or renewal of self, feelings of accomplishment, enhancement of self-image, social interaction and belongingness, and lasting physical products of the activity (e.g., a painting, scientific paper, piece of furniture). A further benefit - self-gratification, or the combination of superficial enjoyment and deep satisfaction - is also one of the main benefits of casual leisure to the extent that the component of enjoyment dominates.[2]

The fifth quality - participants in serious leisure tend to *identify* strongly with their chosen pursuits - springs from the presence of the other five. In contrast, casual leisure, although hardly humiliating or despicable, is nonetheless too fleeting, mundane, and commonplace for most people to find a distinctive identity there. I imagine that this was the quality Cicero had in mind when he coined his famous slogan: *Otium cum dignitate*, or leisure with dignity.

The sixth quality of serious leisure is the *unique ethos* that grows up around each expression of it. A central component of this ethos is the special social world that develops when enthusiasts in a particular field pursue their interests in it over many years. Unruh (1979, p. 115) defines the social world as:

> a unit of social organization which is diffuse and amorphous. . . . Generally larger than groups or organizations, social worlds are not necessarily defined by formal boundaries, membership lists, or spatial territory. . . . A social world must be seen as an internally recognizable constellation of actors, organizations, events, and practices which have coalesced into a perceived sphere of interest and involvement for participants. Characteristically, a social world lacks a powerful centralized authority structure and is delimited by . . . effective communication and not territory nor formal group membership.

In a later paper, Unruh (1980) added that social worlds are characterized by voluntary identification, by a freedom to enter into and depart from them. Moreover, because they are so diffuse, it is common for their members to be only partly involved in all the activities they have to offer. After all, a social world may be local, regional, multiregional, national, even international. Third, people in complex societies are often members of several social worlds, only some of which are related to leisure. Finally, social worlds are held together, to an important degree, by semiformal, or "mediated communication." They are rarely heavily bureaucratized, yet because of their diffuseness, they are rarely characterized by intense face-to-face interaction. Rather, communication is typically mediated by newsletters, posted notices, telephone messages, mass mailings, Internet communications, radio and television announcements, and similar means, with the strong possibility that the Internet could become the most popular of these in the future.

Every social world contains four types of members: strangers, tourists, regulars, and insiders (Unruh, 1979; 1980). The strangers are intermediaries who normally participate little in the leisure activity itself, but who nonetheless do something important to make it possible, for example, by managing municipal parks (in amateur baseball), minting coins (in hobbyist coin collecting), and organizing the work of teachers' aids (in career volunteering). Tourists are temporary participants in a social world; they have come on the scene momentarily for entertainment, diversion, or profit. Most amateur and hobbyist activities have publics of some kind, which are, at bottom, constituted of tourists. The clients of many volunteers can be similarly classified. The regulars routinely participate in the social world; in serious leisure, they are the amateurs, hobbyists, and volunteers themselves. The insiders are those among them who show exceptional devotion to the social world they share, to maintaining it, to advancing it. In the studies of amateurs, such people were analyzed as "devotees" and contrasted with "participants," or regulars (Stebbins, 1992, pp. 46-48).

Missing from Unruh's conceptualization of the social world but vitally important for the study of serious leisure, is the proposition that a rich subculture is found there as well, one function of which is to interrelate the "diffuse and amorphous constellations." Consequently, it should be noted that members find associated with each social world a unique set of special norms, values, beliefs, lifestyles, moral principles, performance standards, and similar shared representations. Only by taking these elements into account can we logically speak about, for example, social stratification in social worlds, as Unruh does when distinguishing insiders from regulars and I have done in serious leisure by distinguishing devotees, who arc highly dedicated to their pursuit, from participants, who are moderately dedicated to it (Stebbins, 1992, p. 46).

In addition to my own work, empirical validation of these six distinctive qualities comes from several studies (e.g., Parker, 1996; McQuarrie & Jackson, 1996; Siegenthaler and Gonsalez, 1997; Nichols and King, 1999; Arai, in press).

Careers

Exploratory research on careers in serious leisure has so far proceeded from a broad, rather loose definition: a leisure career is the typical course, or passage, of a type of amateur, hobbyist, or volunteer that carries the person into and through a leisure role and possibly into and through a work role. The essence of any career, whether in work, leisure, or elsewhere, lies in the temporal continuity of the activities associated with it. Moreover, we are accustomed to thinking of this continuity as one of accumulating rewards and prestige, as progress along these lines from some starting point, even though continuity may also include career retrogression. Serious leisure careers have been empirically examined in my own research and that of Baldwin and Norris (1999).

The essence of career lies in the temporal continuity of the activities associated with it. It is common to think of this continuity as one of accumulating rewards and prestige, as progress along these lines from some starting point. But continuity may also include career retrogression. In the worlds of sport and entertainment, for instance, athletes and artists may reach performance peaks early on, after which the prestige and rewards diminish as the limelight shifts to younger, sometimes more capable practitioners.

Career continuity may occur predominantly within, between, or outside organizations. Careers in organizations such as a community orchestra or hobbyist association only rarely involve the challenge of the "bureaucratic crawl," to use the imagery of C. Wright Mills. In other words, little or no hierarchy exists for them to climb. Nevertheless, the amateur or hobbyist still gains a profound sense of continuity, and hence career, from his or her more or less steady development as a skilled, experienced, and knowledgeable participant in a particular form of serious leisure and from the deepening satisfaction that accompanies this kind of personal growth. Some volunteer careers are intraorganizational as well.

Still, many amateurs and volunteers as well as some hobbyists have careers that bridge two or more organizations. For them, career continuity stems from their growing reputations as skilled, knowledgeable practitioners and, based on this image, from finding increasingly better leisure opportunities available through various outlets (as in different teams, orchestras, organizations, tournaments, exhibitions, journals, conferences, contests, shows, and the like). Meanwhile, still other amateurs and hobbyists, who pursue noncollective lines of leisure (e.g., tennis, painting, clowning, golf, entertainment magic), are free of even this marginal affiliation with an organization. The extraorganizational career of the informal volunteer, the forever willing and sometimes highly skilled and knowledgeable helper of friends, relatives, and neighbors is of this third type.

The serious leisure participants who stick with their activities eventually pass through four, possibly five career stages: beginning, development, establishment, maintenance, and decline. But the boundaries separating these stages are imprecise, for as the condition of continuity suggests, the participant passes largely imperceptibly from one to the next. The beginning lasts as long as is necessary for interest in the activity to take root. Development begins when the interest has taken root and its pursuit becomes more or less routine and systematic. Serious leisure participants advance to the establishment stage once they have moved beyond the requirement of having to learn the basics of their activity. During the maintenance stage, the leisure career is in full bloom; here participants are now able to enjoy to the utmost the pursuit of it, the uncertainties of getting established having been put behind them, for the most part. By no means all serious leisure participants face decline, but those who do, experience it because of deteriorating mental or physical skills. A more detailed description of the career framework and its five stages is available elsewhere (Stebbins, 1992, chap. 5; on hobbies see Stebbins, 1996).

Costs, Rewards, and Motivation

Both implicitly and explicitly much of serious leisure theory rests on the following proposition: to understand the meaning of such leisure for those who pursue it is in significant part to understand their motivation for the pursuit. Moreover, one fruitful approach to understanding the motives that lead to serious leisure participation is to study them through the eyes of the participants who, past studies reveal (Stebbins, 1992, chap. 6; 1996a; 1998b; Arai & Pedlar, 1997), see it as a mix of offsetting costs and rewards experienced in the central activity. The rewards of this activity tend to outweigh the costs, however, the result being that the participants usually find a high level of personal satisfaction in them.

The history of the social psychology of leisure shows that psychologists have largely ignored the subjective side of leisure motivation, the meaning of particular leisure activities for those who engage in them. The closest these specialists have come to embracing this perspective is to differentiate its intrinsic and extrinsic forms. According to Neulinger (1981, p. 31),

> if the satisfaction gained stems from the activity and not from a payoff or consequence therefrom, the behavior is judged to be intrinsically motivated. If the satisfaction comes from a payoff - if the activity itself is not the reward but only leads to a reward - then the activity is seen as extrinsically motivated. One engages in extrinsically motivated behavior *in order to* [italics in the original].

Neulinger adds that certain activities are driven by both forms of motivation. Thus, although most work is extrinsically motivated and nearly all leisure is intrinsically motivated, exceptions exist on both sides. Some work is so absorbing that its devotees voluntarily seek additional amounts of it; in this kind of work, including some professional work, the line separating it from leisure is virtually erased. And an element of extrinsic motivation is found in leisure where, for example, participants strive to make money from a pastime or hope to be deeply appreciated for helping people in need.

But how do people view their own motives for participating in particular leisure activities? The psychology of leisure needs and motivation has only recently begun to consider their point of view. In 1989, Mannell (1989, p. 286) observed that psychological research, while confirming the general existence of leisure satisfaction, had so far failed to identify "the most meaningful and appropriate factors that might affect the quality of . . . [that] satisfaction." In other words, psychologists were assuming rather than empirically studying the link between leisure satisfaction, on the one hand, and particular leisure activities and their settings, on the other. At the same time, they had learned that people do see their leisure in general as intrinsically rewarding, as relatively unconstrained activity they initiate for their own satisfaction.

Today, we know considerably more about the link between leisure satisfaction and particular leisure activities. Mannell and Kleiber (1997, pp. 208-209) provide a review of some of the research in this area, most of which, however, centers on casual leisure. Meanwhile, serious leisure research can also make a significant contribution here, founded as much of it has been on the use of qualitative methods for the direct exploration of particular amateur, hobbyist, and volunteer activities. Using this approach has led to the discovery of a distinctive set of rewards for each activity examined (Stebbins, 1992, 1996a, 1998b; Arai & Pedlar, 1997). In these studies the participant's leisure satisfaction has been found to stem from a constellation of particular rewards gained from the activity, whether playing music, collecting stamps, or teaching crafts to the elderly. Furthermore, these rewards are not only satisfying in themselves, but also satisfying as counterweights to the costs encountered in the activity.

That is, every serious leisure activity contains its own costs - a distinctive combination of tensions, dislikes and disappointments - which each participant confronts in his or her own way. For instance, a volunteer board member may not always feel like attending board meetings, occasionally have his or her ideas rejected when there, be asked to perform a disagreeable task from time to time, and still regard this activity as highly satisfying - as (serious) leisure - because it also offers certain powerful rewards. Put more precisely, then, the drive to gain satisfaction in serious leisure is the drive to experience the rewards of a given leisure activity, such that its costs are seen by the participant as more or less insignificant by comparison. This is at once the meaning of the activity for the participant and his or her motivation for engaging in it. It is this motivational sense of the concept of reward that distinguishes it from the idea of durable benefit set out earlier, an idea that emphasizes outcomes rather than antecedent conditions. Nonetheless, the two ideas constitute two sides of the same social psychological coin.

The rewards of a serious leisure pursuit are the more or less routine values that attract and hold its enthusiasts. Every serious leisure career both frames and is framed by the continuous search for these rewards, a search that takes months, and in some fields years, before the participant consistently finds deep satisfaction in his or her amateur, hobbyist, or volunteer role. Ten rewards have so far emerged in the course of my various exploratory studies of amateurs, hobbyists, and career volunteers. As the following list shows, these rewards are predominantly personal.

Personal rewards
1. Personal enrichment (cherished experiences)
2. Self-actualization (developing skills, abilities, knowledge)
3. Self-expression (expressing skills, abilities, knowledge already developed)
4. Self-image (known to others as a particular kind of serious leisure participant)
5. Self-gratification (combination of superficial enjoyment and deep satisfaction)[3]
6. Re-creation (regeneration) of oneself through serious leisure after a day's work
7. Financial return (from a serious leisure activity)

Social rewards
8. Social attraction (associating with other serious leisure participants, with clients as a volunteer, participating in the social world of the activity)
9. Group accomplishment (group effort in accomplishing a serious leisure project; senses of helping, being needed, being altruistic)
10. Contribution to the maintenance and development of the group (including senses of helping, being needed, being altruistic in making the contribution)

In my different studies of amateurs, hobbyists, and volunteers, the interviewees, depending on the activity, often gave different weightings to these rewards in order to reflect their importance relative to each other. Moreover, these studies revealed some notable variations among small numbers of individual participants in the same activity. For instance, financial return has been by far the weakest reward in serious leisure for, among the few amateurs and volunteers who have been paid, the remuneration has been too small to contribute significantly to their livelihood. Nevertheless, some common ground exists, for the studies show that, in terms of their personal importance, most serious leisure participants rank self-enrichment and self-gratification as number one and number two, although to find either reward, the participant must have sufficient levels of relevant skill, knowledge, and experience. In other words, self-actualization, which was often ranked third in importance, is also highly rewarding in serious leisure.

I have followed the same procedure throughout, which has been to ask each interviewee first to examine a list of the aforementioned rewards (printed on a file card) and then to rank them from highest to lowest in terms of personal importance, giving no rank whatsoever to those that fail to apply. After discussing in detail the rewards and their ranking with each respondent, I encouraged him or her, in line with the exploratory mission of the study, to add other rewards to the list, if they could think of any. This is how the list grew and some of the rewards came to be reconceptualized. To determine the ranks for an entire sample, weights were first assigned to the ranked rewards of each respondent and, to construct a collective profile, the weighted ranks were then summed up for each reward for the subsample in question.

As several scholars have recently argued (Codina, 1999; Harries & Currie, 1998; Siegenthaler & Gonsalez, 1997; Lee, Dattilo, & Howard, 1994), serious leisure experiences also have their negative side. In line with this reasoning, I have always asked my respondents to discuss the costs they find in their serious leisure, namely, the dislikes, tensions, and disappointments. So far, it has been impossible to develop a general list of costs as has been done for the rewards, since the costs tend to be highly specific to each serious leisure activity. Thus each activity studied to date has been found to have its own constellation of costs, but as the respondents see them, they are invariably and heavily outweighed in importance by the rewards of the activity.

Motivation to pursue serious leisure has also been found to be related to identity. Laverie's (1998) research on participation in fitness activity suggests that motivation to engage in serious leisure is related to the level of identity salience of particular activities. That is, the lower the salience of a given activity the lower the motivation to participate in it.

Serious Leisure in the Community

Serious leisure participants pursue their activities in a particular institutional milieu, which facilitates, constrains, and even reacts to their actions there. To be precise, participants engage in serious leisure primarily within the confines of their society's institution of leisure, although their activities may overlap or intersect with the institutions of work and the family as well.

I have used the term "family" throughout my research on serious leisure as an umbrella term for all steady, cohabitational relationships with a member of the same or the opposite sex, whether children are present and whether the relationships are solemnized in a marriage ceremony. Data from my research indicate that relationships like boyfriend-girlfriend or fiancé-fiancée are the least complicated and problematic of all the possible family ties. Here the relationship is likely to founder unless one partner fully accepts, or at least tolerates, the other partner's leisure passion. Although different serious leisure activities generate different familial tensions among married couples and their families, the general conclusion of these studies is that immediate family members, including children, generally accept the pursuit that inspires the participant, despite the tensions it sometimes creates.

Turning to work, my studies show that it comes first in any showdown with serious leisure. They also show that serious leisure involvements often ebb and flow over the adult years. Individual participants struggle to balance work and leisure commitments with the condition of limited time ever in the background. Serious leisure activities usually take place during evenings and weekends, which accommodates the conventional nine-to-five, Monday-to-Friday employment schedule. This arrangement results in the occasional full and hectic day for some participants, although at least they can have their leisure cake and eat it too, as it were. In short, leisure-work conflict has so far been a problem for only a minority of serious leisure participants. Nevertheless, this conflict could become more widespread should more people start working evenings or weekends.

Finally, I have argued over the years that amateurs and the activities they pursue are marginal in society, for amateurs are neither dabblers nor professionals (see also Stebbins, 1979). Moreover, the studies of hobbyists and career volunteers show that they are just as marginal and for many of the same reasons (Stebbins, 1996a, 1998b). Several properties of serious leisure give substance to these observations. One, although seemingly illogical according to common sense, is that serious leisure is characterized empirically by an important degree of positive commitment to a pursuit (Stebbins, 1992, pp. 51-52). This commitment is measured, among other ways, by the sizeable investment of time and energy in the leisure made by its devotees and participants.[4] Two, serious leisure is pursued with noticeable intentness, with such passion that Erving Goffman (1963) once qualified amateurs and hobbyists as the "quietly disaffiliated."[5]

Three, serious leisure tends to be uncontrollable; it engenders in its practitioners the desire to engage in the activity beyond the time and money available for it. Whereas some casual leisure can also be uncontrollable, our marginality hypothesis implies that this proclivity is generally significantly stronger among serious leisure participants. Four, amateurs in particular occupy the status of peripheral member of the profession on which they model their activities, while nevertheless being judged in their execution of those activities by the standards of that same profession.

The idea of marginality used here differs from the kind of marginality afflicting the "marginal man," a conception pioneered many years ago by sociologists for describing the lifestyles of immigrants. The latter are marginal because, in the typical case, they are caught between two cultures, such that their marginality becomes a way of life, a condition touching nearly every corner of their existence. Although this ethnic marginality and the leisure marginality on which the present chapter focuses are both centered on peripheral and ambiguous social statuses, the second kind of marginality is hardly as pervasive as the first. Rather, leisure marginality is a segmented and therefore limited marginality associated with certain uncommon or unusual statuses.

In leisure marginality, as in ethnic marginality, we find among the status incumbents themselves as well as in the wider community an *ambiguity*, or a lack of clarity, as to who these incumbents, these marginal people, really are and what they really do. The studies I conducted on amateurs, hobbyists, and volunteers revealed the multifaceted nature of this ambiguity. On the cultural side, ambiguity is manifested both narrowly as a conflict of expectations and broadly as a conflict of values (e.g., on commitment to special interests and rewards, Stebbins, 1992, chap. 7). On the relational side, incongruent status arrangements develop, as when amateurs in pursuit of their leisure goals help professionals reach their work goals. On the psychological side, practitioners may become ambivalent toward their serious leisure as they confront their own marginality during the many and diverse expressions of this ambiguity in everyday life. The following episode taken from the baseball study exemplifies the psychological ambiguity inherent in serious leisure:

> One father arrived at a late Sunday afternoon practice with his two young boys: "My wife had to be away this afternoon," he commented. "She said you watch them or stay home." He had to leave the field several times during the workout to break up a fight between them or soothe a minor injury incurred while scampering around the bleachers and surrounding area (Stebbins, 1979, p. 220).

In summing up these ideas about ambiguity, it is evident that both the practitioners of a serious leisure activity and the larger society are inclined to see it as marginal to the main problems around which the social institutions of work, family, and leisure have developed as well as to the principal ways people use to try to solve those problems.

My research in all three types of serious leisure demonstrates that family and work and even other leisure activities pull serious leisure practitioners in two, if not three, directions at once, making time demands that together often exceed the total available hours. In addition, unlike family and work activities where institutional supports sustain serious involvement, such support for equivalent activities in leisure is absent. For example, such widely accepted values as providing for one's family, working hard on the job, or being family centered - all of which help to justify our efforts in these spheres - are simply lacking in most serious leisure.[6] Moreover, their very existence in the institutions of family and work threatens serious leisure involvement elsewhere by reducing the importance of the latter while enhancing that of the former.

Most critical, however, is the observation that serious leisure practitioners are marginal even to the institution of leisure itself. That is, they implicitly or explicitly reject a number of the values, attitudes, and patterns of behavior constituting the very core of modern leisure, which is casual leisure. For instance, many an interviewee told me about his or her feeble interest in television or in such passive leisure as frivolous talk and people watching. Like marginal people everywhere, then, those who go in for serious leisure lack key institutional supports for their goals as well as for their personal and collective ways of reaching them.

Marginal statuses are common in industrial societies, where rapid social change gives birth to new forms of work and leisure. Still, as time passes in these societies, certain forms do become less, sometimes even much less, ambiguous and marginal.[7] A few of them may even become central. Nevertheless, according to the studies referred to in this book, such a transformation has failed to occur in the field of serious leisure. Furthermore, it appears unlikely to occur there for some time.

Lifestyle, Identity, and Central Life Interest

We turn next to three additions to the basic perspective made since 1991. The first of these is lifestyle. That people find special lifestyles associated with the leisure worlds they inhabit went unrecognized until after I wrote the 1992 statement. Since then, however, it has become clear that not only do serious leisure activities generate their own lifestyles, but that they also generate their own identities, both being centered on a particular form of leisure considered by the participants as a central life interest.

Dictionary definitions, which tend to conceive of lifestyle simply as a way of living, are for the most part circular and hence of little use in the present discussion. Social science definitions have advanced well beyond this truism. "A lifestyle is a distinctive set of shared patterns of tangible behavior that is organized around a set of coherent interests or social conditions or both, that is explained and justified by a set of related values, attitudes, and orientations and that, under certain conditions, becomes the basis for a separate, common social identity for its participants" (Stebbins, 1997b). Note that this definition refers exclusively to collective lifestyles. This restriction is not to deny the existence of idiosyncratic, highly personal, lifestyles led by recluses, workaholics, people suffering from acute mental disorder, and other loners. Rather the restriction recognizes that, to this point, the study of lifestyles has concentrated almost entirely on shared patterns of tangible behavior, leaving us with little information about individual lifestyles (Veal, 1993).

According to the foregoing definition, some lifestyles offer their participants a special social identity. In other words, the participants are members of a category of humankind who recognize themselves and, to some extent, are recognized by the larger community for the distinctive mode of life they lead. Prostitutes, beach habitués, travelling sales people, and the institutionalized elderly are identifiable in many ways, possibly the most visible being their peculiar lifestyles. The same can be said for the enthusiasts pursuing many of the serious leisure activities.

A profound lifestyle awaits anyone who routinely pursues a serious leisure career in, say, amateur theater, volunteer work with the mentally handicapped, the hobby of model railroading, or that of mountain climbing. And it is possible that this person also finds exciting, albeit clearly less profound, lifestyles in such casual leisure pastimes as socializing in hot tubs and "whooping it up" at weekend beer parties. But many other forms of casual leisure, for example routine people watching and strolling in the park, are usually not shared with large numbers of other people and therefore cannot be considered lifestyles according to the preceding definition. Moreover, in themselves, these activities are too superficial and unremarkable to serve as the basis for a recognizable mode of living.

To the extent that lifestyles form around complicated, absorbing, satisfying activities, as they invariably do in serious leisure, they can also be viewed as behavioral expressions of the participants' central life interests in those activities. In his book by the same title, Robert Dubin (1992) defines this interest as "that portion of a person's total life in which energies are invested in both physical/intellectual activities and in positive emotional states." Sociologically, a central life interest is often associated with a major role in life. And since they can only emerge from positive emotional states, obsessive and compulsive activities can never become central life interests.

Dubin's (1992, pp. 41-42) examples clearly establish that either work or serious leisure can become a central life interest:

> A workaholic is an individual who literally lives and breathes an occupation or profession. Work hours know no limits, and off-work hours are usually filled with work-related concerns. Nothing pleases a workaholic more than to be working. Such an individual has a CLI [central life interest] in work.[8]
>
> A dedicated amateur or professional athlete will devote much more time and concentration to training than will be invested in actual competition. Over and over again athletes will practice their skills, hoping to bring themselves to a peak of performance. Even though practicing may be painful, the ultimate competitive edge produced by practice far outweighs in satisfaction and pride any aches and pains of preparation. Such people make their athletic life their CLI.
>
> A committed gardener, stamp collector, opera buff, jet setter, cook, housewife, mountain climber, bird watcher, computer "hacker," novel reader, fisherman, or gambler (and you can add many more to the list from your own experiences) are all usually devoted to their activity as a central life interest.

> Give such individuals a chance to talk freely about themselves and they will quickly reveal their CLI through fixation on the subject and obvious emotional fervor with which they talk about it.

These are hobbyist and amateur activities. But career volunteers find a lively central life interest in their pursuits, too:

> In American politics, and probably the politics of most Western countries, groups increasingly enter political life with a single issue as their rallying point. That single issue may be taxes, abortion, women's rights, the environment, consumerism, conservatism, or civil rights, and much activity and emotion is invested in "the movement." Adherents come to view themselves as personifying "good guys" who rally around a movement's single issue, making their movement their CLI.

As happens with leisure lifestyle, a leisure identity also arises in parallel with a person's leisure-based central life interest. In other words, that person's lifestyle in a given serious leisure activity gives expression to his or her central life interest there while forming the basis for a personal and community identity as some one who goes in for that activity.

Serious Leisure and Leisure Studies

Because it is distinguished by an unusual quality, serious leisure occupies a unique place as a research area in the broader field of leisure studies. That quality is the fundamentally *populist* character of serious leisure; it is an activity pursued by ordinary people who recognize it as special. That I, a social scientist, coined the term "serious leisure" to designate this activity and not the participants themselves in no way belies this basic point. Put otherwise, this concept, unlike "the great majority of concepts . . . currently used in leisure studies" (Jackson & Burton, 1989, p. 11), comes from outside the social science disciplines composing this research domain. Such an origin - there are no conceptual roots in any particular discipline - firmly establishes serious leisure as an interdisciplinary field, defined here as an approach that attempts to combine or interlace the knowledge of different branches of research (Burdge, 1989, p. 30). To this end, the theoretical and empirical work in this area has advanced to the point where it can be classified according to five somewhat overlapping and interconnected levels of analysis.

The first level - *personal* - is the province of psychology and social psychology. Motivation (including the analysis of costs and rewards), commitment, self-conception, personal values, personal well-being, and lifelong and self-directed learning number among the objects of research here. Conceptual and empirical work explicitly linking these ideas with serious leisure or one of its types has been undertaken in Israel, England, Canada, and the United States (e.g., Shamir, 1988; Yair, 1990; Buchanan, 1985; Haworth, 1986; Haworth & Hill, 1992; Iso-Ahola, 1989; Gross, 1982, pp. 8, 68; Siegenthaler & Lam, 1992; Carpenter, Patterson, & Pritchard, 1990; Mannell, 1993; Stebbins, 1992a: chap. 6; Stebbins, 1992b). In addition, Hamilton-Smith (1992) has observed that serious leisure offers an avenue by which we may experience optimal psychological arousal, a psychological state generated through such processes as play, exploration, and aesthetic appreciation.

The *interactional* level is the more or less exclusive province of social psychology. Here research and theory are concerned with the ways in which participants interact with each other while engaging in serious leisure and with nonparticipants while arranging to do so. Participants also interact with the publics of their activities, their clients (in career volunteering), and their professional counterparts (in amateurism). As my studies show, amateurs are sometimes forced to negotiate the time they need for their leisure with such people as spouses and employers who have special claims on that time. I have also learned that serious leisure, whatever its type, can stir up a lively conversation with spouses, friends, or relatives. Thus, the study of interaction in serious leisure occasionally gets extended into the spheres of work and family. All the ethnographically oriented field research considered in the 1992 synthesis provides data on the social interaction characteristic of the serious leisure under study. Outside my own work, however, only a handful of interactional studies have been explicitly guided by the concept of serious leisure or one of its types (e.g., Fine, 1987; Olmsted, 1988; Shamir, 1988; Yair, 1990).

Anthropology joins social psychology and the moderately abstract levels of sociology on the *mesostructural* level. "Mesostructure" is David Maines's (1982) term for the level of analysis found between the levels of direct social interaction and abstract formations of community and society. Here we find research on such structures as small groups and social networks, as well as on what Hall (1987) calls "collective activity," or the coordinated sequences of acts carried out by two or more persons in relation to certain goals (e.g., executing a play in hockey, making music in an orchestra). The concept of the "social world," identified earlier as one of the defining qualities of serious leisure, is located here. Finally, the study of leisure lifestyles, whether casual or serious, is perhaps most accurately conceived of as belonging to this level of analysis. Ethnographically oriented studies typically contain a number of mesostructural observations.

The contribution of anthropology to the study of serious leisure is potentially great, even if still largely unrealized. Ruth Finnegan's (1989) detailed analysis of the multitude of music worlds in Milton Keynes, England, is a rare contribution from this discipline. Indeed, a number of disciplines could become involved at this level, as suggested by Gates's (1991) imaginative application in the United States of the serious leisure perspective to explain variations in the propensity to participate in music, a prominent research problem in music education. He found that such participation often takes place in small groups.

The *structural* level of analysis centers on the development, maintenance, and change of abstract social (rather than concrete interpersonal) relationships between serious leisure participants and between them and the wider community and society. This is the domain of anthropology, sociology, and history; in the main it encompasses the relationships between amateurs and professionals, amateurs and hobbyists and their publics, and volunteers and their clients as well as the functionaries who direct the former. The objects of study on this level include roles and their interrelationships in large-scale organizations, social movements, and social systems, as well as various forms of community and societal organization. The process of reciprocal cause and effect is evident here as these structures affect the people who participate in serious leisure and, in turn, are affected by them.

Furthermore, there is invariably a rich history surrounding the development of every reasonably well-established form of serious leisure. In the fields I studied, this history was generally available in various written documents, although further data collection was sometimes required to adapt it to my research interests. Yet, it was not until the study of entertainment magicians (Stebbins, 1993a, chap. 1) that I truly learned how to make the history an integral part of my structural and sociocultural analyses of the field I was studying. Thankfully, the magicians themselves talked so much about the history of magic that I could scarcely ignore it. Of course, the history of a field of serious leisure can be studied for its own sake, as did Ainley (1980) in ornithology, Lankford (1981a; 1981b) and Rothenberg (1981) in astronomy, Riedler (1992) in barbershop singing, and Gelber (1992, 1997) in stamp collecting and the various do-it-yourself hobbies.

Most ethnographic studies of serious leisure contain a certain amount of structural analysis, even if mesostructural and interactional analyses tend to predominate. Stanley Parker's (1987) short essay on British peace volunteers exemplifies well the structural approach to the study of serious leisure. Finnegan (1989) works from a structural perspective at several points in her study of the music scene in Milton Keynes.

The *sociocultural* level of analysis complements the preceding level by introducing additional perspectives from history, sociology, and anthropology as well as drawing on various perspectives in philosophy. It is chiefly on this level, I believe, that geography will contribute to the study of serious leisure, if and when the idea catches on there. The shared values, norms, beliefs, customs, and patterns of behavior - all being main elements of culture - are, as it were, the nuts and bolts holding together the structure of abstract relationships of each world of serious leisure. For instance, the behavior patterns expressing the ways we use time have been the object of considerable research in the leisure sciences. In this regard, Phillip Bosserman (1993) found, in the sole study of time use in serious leisure, that many barbershop singers are frustrated because they lack the hours they need to pursue their hobby to the extent they would like.

Furthermore, the sociocultural level is where one can carry out institutional analyses, such as those centered on the mesh of leisure with family and work (which can be problematic), the marginality of serious leisure (Stebbins, 1992a, pp. 55-57, 120-122; Stebbins, 1996a), and the relationship of serious to casual leisure. Eliot Freidson (1978) concluded that amateurs and volunteers produce a significant proportion of the goods and services in modern societies which, however, never find expression in the list of official indicators of the economy and the goods and services market. Finally, let us not forget a sociocultural question of growing importance: what is the value of serious leisure for people who are unemployed, unconventionally employed (e.g., four-day workweeks, job sharing, contractual work), and retired (Stebbins, 1992a, pp. 127-133)? The answer to this question is taken up in chapter 9.

This is also the level where we can pursue such philosophical and quasi-philosophical questions as the nature of the benefits that accrue to the community and the larger society when some of its members are attracted to serious leisure (see Stebbins, 1992a, pp. 118-120). What is the value of such leisure from the standpoint of social well-being, or the well-being of society? Is leisure in general a modern social problem, as I once argued (Stebbins, 1980a), the suggested remedy for which is that people take up some sort of serious leisure? Michael Litner (1992) draws our attention to the ethical consequences of the leisure we choose. In this regard, the self-interested pursuit of amateur and hobbyist activities sometimes generates charges of selfishness from the people adversely affected by the participant's drive to engage in those activities, a matter about which more will be said in chapter 6. Meanwhile, the philosophical nature of altruism in volunteer work begs further scrutiny. Robert Wuthnow (1991, pp. 36-39, 222-225) briefly considers it with regard to volunteerism and charity (for a general sociological exploration of altruism, self-interestedness, and selfishness, see Stebbins, 1981b). Finally, the policy implcations of serious leisure, about which next to nothing has been written, finds its taxonomic place on this level of analysis.

Conclusions

From the broadest perspective, serious leisure can be seen as both a type of leisure and a form of leisure experience, which is how it is treated in this book. Hamilton-Smith (1992, pp. 247-48) has reviewed the literature centering on the experience dimension. Analyses of leisure made from this angle, he says, appear to date from the ideas of John Neulinger (1974), who saw leisure as intrinsically motivated, and B.L. Driver (1970), who examined it from a humanistic perspective. Hamilton-Smith (1992: 247) describes the experience dimension. "It generally assumes that leisure is characterised by such qualities as freedom of choice, freedom from external control or constraint, intrinsic satisfaction and a sense of involvement. This position also generally assumes that leisure is good in itself and a desirable state of being."

Leisure can be studied from many angles, however, with experience being but one of them. Consequently, this book will contain relatively little about the time dimension of leisure, which is typically studied in objective terms, as in the different uses of time - working time and free time - and the relative distributions and proportions of each as calculated for an entire society or one or more of its segments. Philosophically, leisure, often in comparison with work, can be examined, as it has been for hundreds of years, according to its necessity, desirability, and ethicality. Thus the analysis of leisure in general and serious leisure in particular as distinctive forms of experience helps us understand only one facet, albeit an important facet, of the institution and its set of activities that goes by this name.

Chapter 2

The Liberal Arts Hobbies

The 1992 literature review and theoretical elaboration of the research done since the mid-1970s concentrated mainly on amateurs, entirely because research on hobbyists and career volunteers from the serious leisure perspective was comparatively rare. Moreover, this review examined only four of the five categories of hobbyist: the collectors, makers and tinkerers, activity participants, and players of sports and games. Among other things, it revealed that, thanks to Olmsted, the collector had been the type of hobbyist most frequently studied to that point (see, Olmsted 1988, 1991, 1993; Olmsted and Horna, 1989), whereas serious leisure studies of the other three types had been scarcer (but see Bishop and Hoggett, 1986; Parker, 1993).

The review and elaboration also made possible a comparison of the various studies of hobbyists and amateurs which, in turn, brought to light a major gap in the basic taxonomy of these two types. The taxonomy had since the 1970s undergirded the serious leisure perspective and oriented the empirical work carried out in its name. During the review, however, I began to sense that something important was missing. I had neglected to develop a place in the perspective for those who, in their leisure, systematically and fervently seek knowledge for its own sake. What was missing was unambiguous recognition of the *liberal arts hobbies*.

In the present chapter, I set out a framework for filling this theoretical gap, a framework that emerged in the course of exploring the domain of the liberal arts hobby. In particular, the chapter introduces, explains, and elaborates the following assertion: the free-time pursuit of a liberal art is both a distinct hobby and a distinct subtype of serious leisure. This, a new addition to the basic taxonomy, brings to five the number of subtypes of hobbies.

The empirical foundation for this conceptual exploration comes from three sources. The first is my previously-mentioned longitudinal research project on amateurs and their professional counterparts; it consisted of eight studies in art, science, sport, and entertainment conducted between 1974 and 1989 (synthesized in Stebbins, 1992a). Here I began to realize that some of my respondents, particularly those in science, but also some in other fields, were significantly more given to reading about their leisure passion than to practicing it, as seen in gathering data, playing a sport, giving a performance). The second source is my position of resource person for the noncredit course on New Orleans that I present every three years as part of the Travel Study Program offered by the Faculty of Continuing Education at the University of Calgary. Between 1980 and 1998 I have taught the course eight times. Its participants receive ten hours of lectures followed by a nine-day, laboratory-like tour of pertinent sites and events in the Crescent City. The third source is my field study of Calgary francophones, people who routinely speak French as either their first or second language (Stebbins, 1994b). One important generalizations to emerge from this study is that, in part, Franco-Calgarians maintain and transmit their language and culture by means of a range of leisure activities, such that the maintenance and transmission take on the qualities of a hobby.

It should be understood, however, that this empirical foundation could never constitute a logical proof. Rather it served in a different capacity, as terrain on which to explore this new type of hobby and generate grounded theory about it (see Glaser and Strauss, 1967). References made here from time to time to this terrain are to be viewed as part of the inductive process of exploration, where concrete cases illustrate certain aspects of the liberal arts hobby as a type, rather than as part of the deductive process of confirmation, where data test a set of hypotheses introduced on an a priori basis for just that purpose.

The Liberal Arts Hobby

As previously noted a liberal arts hobby is the systematic and fervent pursuit during free time of knowledge for its own sake. People who take up such a hobby have as their primary goal the acquisition of a broad knowledge and understanding of, for example, one or more arts, sports, foods, languages, cultures, histories, sciences, philosophies, or literary traditions. A similar goal motivates the inveterate albeit intellectually oriented followers of current politics.[1] All these hobbyists look on the knowledge and understanding they acquire as ends in themselves rather than, as is typical of serious leisure pursuits (Fine, 1989, p. 325), as background, or means to involvement in another hobby or in an amateur activity. When compared with the other hobbies and the various amateur activities, the knowledge acquired is of primary rather than secondary importance.

The liberal arts hobby is set off from other serious leisure pursuits by two of its most basic characteristics: the search for *broad knowledge* of an area of human life and the search for this knowledge for its *own sake*. Broad knowledge stands in contrast to technical knowledge; an admittedly fuzzy distinction, which is based on degree rather than on crisp demarcation. Still we can say that unlike technical, or detailed knowledge, the broad kind is humanizing. Through it we can gain a deep understanding and acceptance of a significant sector of human life (art, food, language, history, etc.) and the needs, values, desires, and sentiments found there. This understanding and acceptance does not necessarily lead, however, to adoption of the sector of life being studied.

Knowledge sought for its own sake implies that its practical application is secondary. Yet liberal arts hobbyists do use the broad knowledge they acquire. As I point out in a later section people enjoy expressing this knowledge, and the expression may be an important avenue by which they maintain and expand it. But this in no way relegates such knowledge to the status of mere accessory, of being a simple means to a more important end. For example, it is generally true that, in the other hobbies and in the amateur and volunteer fields, participants must have certain kinds of knowledge if they are going to produce anything of merit. Thus aspiring stand-up comics avail themselves of various workshops, programs of instruction, and individual tutoring sessions to learn better how to perform comedy (Stebbins, 1990, chap. 5); volunteer youth workers attend sets of weekend training sessions to learn how to provide support for youth club members (Hamilton-Smith, 1971); old car collectors read numerous manuals and related literature to develop their ability to tour, show, and collect cars and parts of cars (Dannefer, 1980).

Likewise, amateur cooks are continually adding to the technical knowledge they need to prepare their meals well. By contrast, the liberal arts hobbyists who are fascinated by, let us say, the oriental cuisines would likely know a great deal about their ingredients, social significance, and methods of cooking, while being comparatively naive in the art of preparing and serving those same cuisines. To the extent that they are exclusively liberal arts hobbyists and not amateur cooks, they will lack the combination of artistry and technical knowledge needed to prepare and serve meals in the cuisines that have stirred their interest.

A third basic characteristic of the liberal arts hobby is the *profundity* of its broad knowledge; that is such knowledge is more than merely entertaining. This characteristic, which is also found in the more technical bodies of knowledge associated with the other forms of serious leisure, is particularly relevant for the current politics hobbyist. While searching for profound news analyses, this hobbyist must constantly work to avoid or at least bracket the primarily entertaining and therefore rarely enlightening broadcasts and analyses of the political news heard on radio and television (Altheide & Snow, 1991, chap. 2). Entertaining but uninformative mass media reports and analyses also afflict liberal arts hobbyists in the areas of art, sport, and science. It is the unfortunate lot of many a liberal arts hobbyist that he or she often has little choice but to rely on these media for information.

Acquiring Knowledge

The liberal arts hobbyist acquires his or her broad knowledge through *active* rather than passive learning, by intentionally seeking the desired ideas. In other words this hobbyist shares the orientation of other hobbyists who, instead of sitting back and waiting for their leisure experiences to come to them, take the initiative to define their own leisure needs and goals. Like other hobbyists, those who pursue a liberal art as leisure typically explain their attraction to it in self-interested terms, pointing for example to a desire to develop their personalities, intellectual capacities, or understanding of life.

These hobbyists can also be qualified as a special category of lifelong learner (Gross, 1977, pp. 15-17): someone who spends a significant part of his or her life in self-directed growth (Knowles, 1975). Some of those who direct their personal growth do so through formal education and especially through one of its increasingly popular variants, adult education. The latter, as Kaplan (1975, p. 262) and Godbey (1990, p. 230) have observed, is often sought for leisure purposes. Godbey (1990, p. 220) points out that "such learning may be a specific leisure skill, such as tennis or flower arranging, or a subject whose study is undertaken as an end in itself such as the history of ancient Egypt." Here the word "school" truly reflects its etymological origins in the Greek and Latin words *skole* and *scola*, both of which mean leisure (Pieper, 1963, p. 20).

My preliminary observations suggest that reading, chiefly in books, magazines, and newspapers, is the principal way in which hobbyists acquire their liberal arts knowledge. Part of my suspicion that I was neglecting an important category of hobbyist, came from rethinking the observation that some of the amateurs I had studied were more interested in reading about their pursuits than executing them. This pattern was most obvious in the study of amateur and professional astronomers. Nevertheless, at the time, I only summarily acknowledged and then naively ignored the "armchair astronomers" (amateurs who read astronomy but do no research) in an analysis (Stebbins, 1980b, p. 35) that concentrated almost exclusively on the observational astronomers (amateurs who actively collect data). Some of the amateur magicians felt the same way. Still many of the inveterate readers in this art also performed occasionally (Stebbins, 1994b, chap. 4), suggesting that amateurs and hobbyists may find time for an allied hobby, namely, the one of acquiring a broad, liberal arts knowledge of their serious leisure pursuit.[2]

An example of this way of combining serious leisure interests is provided by journalist Susan Scott (1993, p. 3). She recently interviewed a male hobbyist (classifiable as a maker) who specializes in preparing Metis family histories. As a parallel activity he reads continuously to expand his considerable liberal arts knowledge of the history and culture of this group of Canadian native peoples.

Reading, Argyle (1992, pp. 116-117) reports after a review of British research, is the most satisfying of all leisure activities for the largest number of people. Even television is not as satisfying for so many people. Nonetheless, for most people, their reading is casual leisure, something akin to the printed version of what they watch on television: they read about spies, detectives, and adventure. Participating in a book club in no way contradicts this observation, for there appears to be little specialization in them, even if members occasionally read some rather profound works (Cole, 1997). Argyle goes on to note that the public library is used mostly by "the more educated people."

Reading can be substantially augmented by viewing or listening to news analyses and film and radio documentaries, listening to audio tapes and live talks, participating directly in activities related to the hobby, or engaging in a combination of these. The first two are self-explanatory and therefore need no further explanation. The third leads us into the world of educational travel. Of the fourteen tourist roles identified by Yiannakis and Gibson (1992, p. 291), only two - the "anthropologist" and the "archaeologist" - are compatible with the definitions of serious leisure and liberal arts hobbyist. The anthropologist tours because he or she enjoys meeting local people, trying their food, and speaking their language. The archaeologist goes on tours to view archaeological sites and ruins as part of his or her historical study of an ancient civilization.

A sizeable number of universities in North America offer noncredit, educational travel courses and programs. Eastern Washington University, for example, has several "Foreign Studies Programs" of one to two weeks in length centering on, for instance, art in Mexico, writing in Ireland, theater in Britain, and culture in Paris. The International Universities organization in Albuquerque, New Mexico, offers overseas "travel study opportunities" in several different languages. My own aforementioned educational travel course on New Orleans consists of an examination of the music, culture, history, and architecture of one of America's most distinct cities. Other courses in that program center on Greece, Russia, Egyptian archaeology, Peruvian ruins, and the Galapagos Islands. Or consider the Elderhostel Program. It is made up of one- to two-week noncredit courses presently offered in over forty countries. It stands as still another example of self-directed education in the liberal arts which, in this case, is especially attractive for retired people.

Whether travel for the purposes of direct participation qualifies as serious leisure depends in part on whether the pursuit of knowledge there is systematic and enduring. Lewis and Brissett (1981) observe that many contemporary vacationers who spend time in a different culture feel they must learn something about it, which does not mean, however, that they consider study of the culture a hobby. A hobby is pursued over many years, not for just two or three weeks of holiday time. The same caution applies to the volunteer vacations described by McMillon (1991), wherein the "vacationers" work without remuneration on projects in park management, trail building, archaeological excavation, reconstruction of historical sites, and the like. Whereas such vacations can last for as long as two years, a person might want to abandon his or her interest in the project when it finally comes to an end. By this time it could have served as a stepping stone to remunerated work or fulfilled the casual leisure interest of sightseeing.

Expressing Knowledge

Even though liberal arts knowledge is valued for its own sake, for its inherent fascination and enjoyment, many hobbyists in this area also want to externalize it in some way. The motivation for doing so is complicated and remains to be studied systematically. It is possible that people find such knowledge prestigious, of interest to others, useful for making conversation, and so on. At this point in our understanding of the liberal arts hobbies, it is nonetheless safe to assume that two processes are at work in the expression of knowledge: One, by externalizing their knowledge of an art, science, or culture, hobbyists in these fields help themselves maintain what they have learned. Two, in the course of externalizing the knowledge, they may see new relationships and meanings in what they already know. Many a high school and university teacher can attest the validity of both processes, having repeatedly seen them in operation.

The processes of maintaining knowledge and discovering new ideas are nowhere more apparent than when we express our capacity to use a foreign language. We learn a foreign language to read in it or speak in it or do both. In the course of the reading and the speaking we further our facility in both areas, whereas if we did neither we would be unlikely to learn the language in any significant measure. It should be clear that this expression is an essential step in the acquisition and maintenance of the language as a personal value, as a form of knowledge in its own right, rather than as a practical or instrumental application of it. For instance, a person might practically apply the language by seeking employment requiring its use. Alternatively, to serve an amateur or hobbyist interest, he or she might read scientific articles or listen to newscasts in it.

Talk appears to be the main way for liberal arts hobbyists to express their knowledge. And since the knowledge was acquired in leisure it is most likely to be expressed in leisure, notably in casual, sociable conversations with friends and relatives. Such talk may be supplemented wherever possible and socially acceptable with other forms of expression, including slides, photographs, and video and audio tape recordings. These might be produced by the hobbyist after, say, having heard a lecture or having returned from an educational travel tour. Perhaps other ways exist, too, these being dependent, in some instances, on the particular hobbyist or amateur talents the practitioner can bring to his or her liberal art. Photography is one obvious application of this sort; others might include writing and painting. For some people one of these arts could be the main vehicle for expressing their liberal arts hobby, with talk serving chiefly as a supplement.

Lifestyle

From what has been said so far about the liberal arts hobbies, it follows that the ways in which knowledge and understanding are acquired and expressed there result in a distinctive set of lifestyles for the hobbyists themselves. These lifestyles have no real equivalent in other forms of leisure, whether serious or casual. This is because the liberal arts hobbies are for the most part individualistic undertakings. With the exception of learning a language, their acquisition rarely requires the hobbyist to enter a social world. Indeed he or she can seldom find one to enter, which is a characteristic distinguishing this hobby from other forms of serious leisure.

People who are learning a new language and hope to advance to a level where they can easily read and talk in it *must* enter in a profound way the social world of the people who are fluent in the language. My research on those Franco-Calgarians for whom French is their second language demonstrated that, as learners, their port of entry into this social world was ordinarily achieved by way of, in the first instance, certain language courses and the institutions offering them. During this phase of learning the language they had only superficial contact with the social world of the city's francophones. Later, based on their increased linguistic fluency, some of these students deepened their involvement in the local francophone social world by frequenting its clubs, bookstores, cinemas, restaurants, travel agencies, and festivals and special events. In turn these contacts produced a small but growing number of French-language friendships, acquaintanceships, and network ties. It also produced for some an opportunity to work as volunteers for one or more francophone services. Other students, who had the time and financial means, achieved the same end by entering a local francophone social world elsewhere in, say, Quebec or France.

Yet language as a liberal arts hobby associated with a well-developed social world is an exception. So far as I can tell all the other liberal arts hobbies are at best only weakly organized according to a social world. They are nevertheless often social; the foregoing section in which we examined the expression of the liberal arts hobbies demonstrates the validity of this assertion. But the manner of acquiring these hobbies is generally individualistic, centering primarily in reading and secondarily in viewing and listening. The closest most of these hobbyists typically come to entering a social world is when, to advance their interests, they take a noncredit course or participate in an educational travel program. But usually they do this only sporadically, if for no other reason than acquiring knowledge in this manner is seldom inexpensive. Moreover, unlike the clubs, restaurants, and bookstores patronized by the foreign-language hobbyists, the courses are evanescent. For this reason alone they make comparatively poor rallying points for those pursuing serious leisure of this type.

In short the lifestyle of many liberal arts hobbyists is, in its acquisition phase, reclusive. Close friends and relatives might even portray them as to some extent antisocial. Still it is likely that these hobbyists would describe themselves and their leisure in more flattering terms such as being peaceful or relaxed. Moreover, we can say that theirs is an exceptionally flexible type of serious leisure. It can be carried out at the convenience of the person, molded around other activities whether obligatory or not, and accommodated to the demands of work and family.[3] Scheduled courses, lectures, and radio and television programs sometimes momentarily override this flexibility, but with reading as the main method of acquisition rigidification of leisure lifestyle for this reason is relatively uncommon.

Serious reading does require a "study" of some kind. The knowledge being acquired is complex and profound; it often takes considerable time to understand it fully and integrate it well with what one already knows. The tendency toward reclusiveness in these hobbies is partly explained by the need "to get away from it all" to think about the many facts and ideas. People without a study would likely find the liberal arts hobbies difficult to pursue effectively and satisfyingly. But all sorts of places can serve as studies; the quiet room at home is perhaps only the most common. The hobbyist can read in a tranquil place in a city park, on a front porch, or at a public library. In the sense intended here it is the absence of significant distraction that makes for a study.

The liberal arts hobbies can be elitist, and in an earlier era were often thought to be exclusively so (e.g., Pieper, 1963, p. 36; Veblen, 1953, p. 252). Still, present-day observations suggest that these hobbies are by no means universally elitist. It is true that participation in some of them requires exceptional financial resources so as to for example travel widely, purchase numerous books, or take a variety of noncredit courses. Given such requirements people with modest incomes are likely to be excluded. But to the extent that these same people can participate by using the public libraries, listening to their radio and television sets, and subscribing to one or two periodicals in their field of interest, the liberal arts hobbies are in reality accessible to a wide range of social classes in the typical Western society. And while on this subject let us not forget the zealous enthusiast who is inclined to spend every extra penny he or she possesses on his or her leisure passion.[4] Even the inherent "intellectual" quality of the liberal arts hobbies may turn out, upon closer examination, to be much less restrictive than we would predict from the stereotype that only the educated elite take an interest in such pursuits. At least past research has, with a few exceptions, discovered a lack of association between social class and many other forms of serious leisure (Stebbins, 1992, p. 112).

Conclusion

The liberal arts hobbies are far from the style of leisure currently being touted by the promoters and enthusiasts of exercise and physical activity. Although people actively participate in these hobbies - that is, they do something on their own initiative - what they do is largely sedentary. True, some of them have other serious or casual leisure interests that do meet the modern ideal of being physically active. But others are inactive, whether by choice because they dislike sport and exercise or by fate because they have a mental or physical disability. For these people a liberal arts hobby may, so far as the realm of leisure is concerned, be their only possible central life interest.

For these reasons, the liberal arts hobbies should be especially attractive to the elderly, although adequate sight and, in some hobbies, hearing are important preconditions for truly enjoyable participation. We will delve more deeply into these questions in chapter 7.

In brief, when considered together, the liberal arts hobbies do appeal to a wide segment of the community. Additionally, they offer a special place in the world of serious leisure for people who are bodily unable or psychologically unwilling to pursue more physically demanding activities. Based on this broad appeal and the previously mentioned ease of financial access to many of these hobbies, they can be accurately described as one of the most democratic types of serious leisure.

Since people who pursue a liberal arts hobby usually interact too infrequently to generate a social world, it is reasonable to conclude that their collective contribution to the wider community will be different from that of the amateurs, career volunteers, and other hobbyists. The latter three, as I have pointed out elsewhere (Stebbins, 1992, pp. 118-120), contribute to the integration of society through the highly evolved social worlds that spring up around their serious leisure. Although the liberal arts hobbyists are in a much poorer position to contribute to societal integration in this important way, they are, however, in a much better position to contribute in another way, a way that is just as important. That is, they contribute through their deep humanistic understanding of the culture and behavior of another category of humankind. As stated in an earlier section of this chapter, humanistic knowledge, unlike technical, or detailed knowledge, begets a deep understanding and acceptance, although not necessarily adoption, of a significant sector of human life (art, food, history, language, etc.), of the needs, values, desires, sentiments, and the like that are found there.

Ovid writes in *Ex Ponto II* that we should "note . . . that a faithful study of the liberal arts humanizes character and permits it not to be cruel." Should the need for one exist, this is the moral justification for pursuing the liberal arts hobbies in modern times, where intolerance and misunderstanding of those who are different from us threaten world stability. Finally, Ovid's words justify research on this neglected subtype of serious leisure. Indeed they would even seem to exhort us to get on with the job.

Chapter 3

Career Volunteering

In recent decades a handful of theorists and researchers both in leisure studies and in the study of voluntarism and citizen participation have argued the proposition that, depending on the writer, volunteering is invariably or frequently a form of leisure. When collected together, however, these observations and studies still leave some critical issues unresolved, including the one of how to reassure volunteer managers that leisure-seeking volunteers will have the commitment and perseverance needed to fill their roles. There is also the issue of the reaction of the financial backers of nonprofit organizations and even the general public to filling important volunteer roles with people they define as primarily motivated by a search for enjoyment? A third issue is whether "leisurely" volunteers are dependable?

This chapter applies the perspective of serious leisure to volunteering, showing that issues such as those just raised can be resolved to the advantage of both individual volunteers and nonprofit organizations. In particular, I take the position that many volunteer roles, because they offer their incumbents special careers and distinctive sets of rewards, can be understood as serious leisure. This perspective applied to volunteering works to negate the proposition that conceiving of volunteering as leisure trivializes volunteering, implying in the extreme case that volunteers are, at bottom, selfish, unreliable, and prone to giving their least effort. Moreover, I argue that volunteers can simultaneously pursue their activities as serious leisure and make substantial contributions both individually and collectively to the functioning of the wider community. Their utility in this regard is recognized in serious leisure theory. The theory states, however, that self-interestedness is their primary reason for volunteering and that they remain mostly unaware of the broader social ramifications of their actions.

In short, the aim here is to define and explain volunteers and volunteering from the perspective of serious leisure and self-interestedness. The result is a broad theoretical statement about leisure volunteering, which is nevertheless limited in that the serious leisure perspective cannot be applied to all types of volunteering.

Leisure and Volunteering: Compatible Concepts

Notwithstanding the relative lack of scholarly attention given to volunteering by leisure studies specialists, making a case for it as leisure poses little logical difficulty. If the word "volunteering" is to remain etymologically consistent with its French and Latin roots, it can only be seen, as all leisure is, as freely chosen activity. Moreover, as with all leisure, leisure volunteering can only be seen as a basically *satisfying*, or rewarding, experience, for otherwise we are forced to posit that so-called volunteers of this kind are somehow pushed into performing their roles by circumstances they would prefer to avoid, a contradiction of terms. The adjectives "satisfying" and "rewarding" are preferred here to such conventional leisure studies terms as "pleasurable" and "enjoyable" as descriptors for the overall experience of volunteering where, notwithstanding certain disagreeable features of the volunteer role, the volunteer finds the activity profoundly attractive on balance (discussed later). And, while it is true that volunteers are paid in rare instances, even beyond the expenses they incur (e.g., three percent of the sample was paid in the study conducted by Blacksell & Phillips, 1994, p. 13), these emoluments are much too small to constitute a livelihood or obligate the person in some way. Finally, it is also true that volunteering normally includes the clear requirement of being in a particular place, at a specified time, to carry out an assigned function. But as Max Kaplan (1960, pp. 22-25) noted years ago, true leisure can be obligated to some extent, although certainly not to the extent typical of work.

This description of the leisure face of volunteering squares well with Jon Van Til's general definition presented in chapter 1. This definition alludes to the two principal motives of volunteering. One is helping others - volunteering as altruism; the other is helping oneself - volunteering as self-interestedness. Examples of the latter include working for a strongly-felt cause or, as we shall see later, working to experience, as serious leisure enthusiasts do everywhere, the variety of social and personal rewards available in volunteering and the leisure career in which they are framed.[1]

Despite the theoretical compatibility of leisure and volunteering, it is relatively rare both in leisure studies and in the study of voluntarism and citizen participation to find the two discussed together. In the first field, possible because volunteering is seen "as somewhat more lofty than . . . the fun and frivolity often associated with leisure" (Henderson, 1984, p. 58), volunteers have for the most part been ignored as subjects of research. The exceptions to this indictment are considered shortly. Researchers in the second field typically look on volunteers as helpers, as people filling a distinct, contributory role in modern society and, more particularly, in certain kinds of organizations. Whether this role is work or leisure or something else seldom stirs much interest.

Volunteering as Leisure Activity

Whether it is leisure studies specialists looking at volunteering or voluntary action specialists looking at leisure, the result has been much the same: Neither field has been inclined to view its own subject matter through the eyes of the other. Still, significant exceptions exist, some of which will be reviewed here to show how the theoretical link between leisure and volunteering has evolved in recent decades.

Some of the earliest theoretical stirrings in this area came from Bosserman and Gagan (1972, p. 115) and David Horton Smith (1975, p. 148) who argued that, at the level of the individual, all leisure activity is voluntary action. More precise statements were made then and somewhat later by Kaplan (1975, p. 394) and Neulinger (1981, p. 19), two leisure studies specialists, who observed in passing how leisure can serve either oneself or other people or both. It is presumed that they had volunteerism in mind. From the side of voluntary action research, Kenneth Boulding (1973, p. 31) theorized that voluntary service borders on leisure, frequently even overlapping it. Alex Dickson (1974, p. xiii) observed that leisure is seen in commonsense as part of voluntary action, and does in fact "carry this spare-time connotation."

Karla Henderson (1981, 1984) examined the leisure component of volunteering both empirically and theoretically. She noted that social scientists ordinarily regard volunteering in the same way as they regard paid work, as having an external, or extrinsic, orientation - the volunteer has a job to complete for the benefit of the community. This contrasts with the view they hold of leisure as oriented by internal, or intrinsic, interests - the participant enjoys the activity for itself and for the self-expression and self-actualization it may engender. Henderson found that her sample of 4-H workers in the United States defined their volunteering as leisure; for them volunteering was part of their leisure world.

A few years later Stanley Parker (1987) reported findings from research on a group of peace workers. He discovered that, whereas they worked as volunteers for the cause of peace, they considered this work part of their leisure. Parker also completed a second study around this time centered on the serious leisure activities of two samples of volunteers, one drawn in Britain, the other drawn in Australia (reported in Parker, 1992). Here he learned that one person in five engaged in some form of activity classifiable as volunteering. Almost invariably, the people sampled described their volunteering as leisure, as primarily rewarding activity and as secondarily helping activity. Their leisure was nonetheless most substantial; in reality it was serious leisure.

While Parker was studying peace workers, Chambré (1987) was examining elderly volunteers. She reached similar conclusions: her respondents also defined their volunteering as leisure activity. Like Henderson, she wrestled with the extrinsic-intrinsic and the altruistic-self-interested dimensions, both of which pervade leisure volunteering. Volunteering is a worklike activity wherein a person accomplishes a task without remuneration. At the same time, the activity, which is freely chosen, provides many a satisfying experience. Chambré (1987, p. 118) found, however, that the motives given by the elderly for taking up a volunteer role differ from those given for continuing in it. Although their sense of altruism often led them to volunteer in the first place, they were highly motivated by the intrinsic satisfaction they found there to continue in this role.

Working from Chambré's conclusion that volunteering is leisure, Fischer and Schaffer (1993, pp, 51, 106-08), set out to explore the patterns of costs and rewards the elderly experience when they participate in this kind of activity. Following a comprehensive review of the current research and case study literature, the authors concluded that certain costs (e.g., time, hazards, inconvenience) are typically offset by numerous special rewards. The rewards include the following: feeling competent to do the volunteer work, sensing ideological congruence with the organization, and being satisfied with the job done (i.e., work is interesting, professional growth is possible, personal skills are used). Self-actualization, self-enrichment, and opportunities for social interaction were also found to be highly appealing (Fischer & Schaffer, 1993, chap. 10). Moreover, it appears that the elderly are not alone in their feelings that volunteering is a highly rewarding form of leisure. Thompson and Bono (1993) found similar sentiments in their sample of volunteer firefighters whose activities fostered self-actualization, group accomplishment, and a special self-image.

The Serious Leisure Perspective

Treating volunteering one principal type of serious leisure leads us to three aspects of the former that students of voluntary action and citizen participation usually acknowledge but seldom examine. First, as observed previously, volunteers are inspired by two main motives, altruism and self-interestedness. As observed earlier, self-interestedness is a cardinal feature of all serious leisure which, when expressed in volunteering, enters into an intricate, but as yet poorly understood, relationship with altruism. Most specialists in voluntary action research would acknowledge that "the volunteer gets something personal out of it too" (e.g., Smith, 1981; Hodgkinson & Weitzman, 1992), even if they tend to skirt the implications of this observation to concentrate their attention on such questions as his or her place in particular service organizations or the contributions he or she makes to the wider community.

Second, to be precise, serious leisure volunteering is *career* volunteering. And it is likely that the motive of self-interestedness often drives the pursuit of such a career more than the motive of altruism, even where a person's altruism prompted him or her to enter the field in the first place (c.f., Chambré, 1987). Of the two, self-interestedness seems to be the stronger motivator encouraging a volunteer to continue in a serious leisure career in voluntary action. This is true in good part because volunteering requires certain skills, knowledge, or training and, at times, two or three of these. As we shall see, their acquisition is highly rewarding.

In this connection, Ross (1990, pp. 20-27) found in his Canadian survey that the overwhelming majority of volunteers regard these acquisitions as important and regard volunteer work as a satisfying and convenient way of expressing them. He grouped the acquired skills and knowledge according to whether they were interpersonal, communications, fund-raising, technical and office, or organizational and managerial. They are substantial enough to engender a career built on their acquisition and on the often difficult process of applying them. By contrast, giving blood, helping distribute flyers, or taking tickets at the performances of the local community theater (discussed later as casual volunteering) can never qualify as this kind of volunteering. They require no significant skill, knowledge, or training in the typical case.

Third, careers and self-interestedness in volunteering are inspired in good part by a person's experiences with the special rewards found in all types of serious leisure. Until recently, these had been most thoroughly examined in volunteer studies by Fischer and Schaffer (1993), albeit only for the elderly. In comparison with their findings, however, my own research on various amateur activities (summarized in

Stebbins, 1992, chap. 6) and on the hobbyist activity of barbershop singing turned up substantially longer lists of rewards, rewards offered by serious leisure in general to those who participate in it. The study of francophone volunteers in Calgary and Edmonton (Stebbins, 1998b) indicates that volunteers also experience these same benefits, although in ways unique to their type of leisure.

The ten rewards that emerged from this serious of investigations were set out in chapter 1. The rewards of a serious leisure pursuit are the more or less routine values that attract and hold its enthusiasts. They constitute the objects of self-interestedness; they are what someone motivated by self-interestedness hopes to achieve through volunteer work. A given serious leisure career both frames and is framed by this enduring search for rewards, for it takes months, even years, to consistently find deep satisfaction in an amateur, hobbyist, or volunteer role. Note, too, that, in this scheme, being altruistic is conceived of as a reward, as a particular expression of self-enrichment. This suggests that career volunteers can be distinguished from other types of serious leisure participants by the exceptional number of enriching experiences they gain by way of altruistic action.

The rewards presented earlier were phrased in general terms. Nevertheless, research on all three types of serious leisure indicates that participants feel the rewards in special ways unique to their pursuits. Thus, the personal enrichment gained from working with autistic children will not be the same as that gained from coaching adolescent hockey players. Likewise, self-actualization in these two areas proceeds along the lines of the different skills, abilities, and forms of knowledge required by each field. In this regard, the pattern of rewards experienced by career volunteers may diverge from the general pattern described in chapter 1. There it was noted that most serious leisure participants rank the rewards of self-enrichment and enjoyment as number one and two in terms of their personal importance, after which there is with descending rank increasing variation from one activity to the next. The francophone volunteers ranked self-enrichment first, but they ranked group accomplishment second (see also Arai & Pedlar, 1997).

Returning to the question of the sense of satisfaction in serious leisure and career volunteering, it is evident that it, too, is defined in particular terms, through the experience of these rewards. Furthermore, these rewards are not only satisfying in themselves, but also satisfying in their cumulative effect as a counterweight to the costs experienced in the activity. Thus a volunteer board member might not always feel like attending board meetings, occasionally have his or her ideas rejected when there, be asked to perform some disagreeable tasks, and still regard this activity as satisfying - as leisure - because of certain powerful rewards it offers. To sum up, when we speak of self-interestedness in serious leisure and career volunteering, we speak more specifically about gaining satisfaction and experiencing rewards as these substantially offset costs.

Since there has been a great deal of research on the reasons for volunteering and joining voluntary associations (see Bonjean, Markham, & Macken, 1994, for a review), it is in order to ask what the scheme of rewards presented in this book contributes to this area of inquiry. One contribution has already been noted: altruism and self-interestedness have been integrated in a common framework. Another contribution is terminological consistency: the concepts of reward, value, career, altruism, satisfaction, and self-interestedness cohere within the overarching perspective of serious leisure. Third, this perspective and its list of rewards help explain volunteering as a career.

When Volunteering is Serious Leisure

Volunteering, whether formal or informal (Fischer & Schaffer, 1993, p. 30), often carries with it a clear obligation to be at a particular place, at a specified time, to perform a certain function. Yet career volunteering appears to engender no greater load of commitments than many other serious leisure pursuits. Serious leisure participants can be obligated, for example, to attend rehearsals and perform in the next concert of the community orchestra, play for their team in an upcoming game in the local industrial baseball league, or go to the neighborhood primary school at four o'clock two days a week to help children with reading problems. What makes this kind of leisure fundamentally nonobligatory is the following condition: these musicians, athletes, and volunteers can terminate such involvements with relative ease. Having met all proximal obligations, these participants are free to announce their unavailability for any number of future projects. True leisure, including career volunteering, contains a substantial degree of choice.

Moreover, as with other types of serious leisure, career volunteering brings on the occasional need to persevere. Participants who want to continue experiencing the same level of satisfaction in the activity have to meet certain challenges from time to time (sometimes defined as costs). Thus, the aforementioned musicians must practice assiduously to master difficult musical passages, the baseball players must throw repeatedly to perfect their favorite pitches, and the volunteers must search their imaginations for new approaches with which to help children with reading problems. Perseverance can also lead to the realization of such rewards as self-actualization and self-expression. At times, in all three types of serious leisure, the deepest satisfaction comes at the end of the activity rather than during it. To repeat, all participants experience their serious leisure as a substantially favorable balance of costs and rewards, where the second significantly outweigh the first (on this balance among elderly volunteers, see Fischer & Schaffer, 1993, pp. 200-201).

Because formal volunteers often perform tasks delegated to them by a superior or someone else, much of their work is other-directed rather than self-directed (Stebbins & Parker, 1994). Again, this condition might seem to contradict the propositions that volunteering is leisure activity and that such activity is controlled by the participant. Nevertheless, the volunteer is hardly the only type of leisure participant to be directed by someone else. Some amateur and hobbyist activities are other-directed (e.g., orchestra musicians, football players); they stand in contrast with the self-directed variety (e.g., stamp collectors, mountain climbers). In part, the satisfaction of other-directed leisure results from the rewards of collective accomplishment and the attractiveness of working with other people, both of which are framed in the realization that someone has to coordinate the actions of the parts if all are to experience a gratifying whole.

What marks leisure volunteering as a special type of serious leisure is its altruism, which invariably propels it. A significant part of what is rewarding and hence leisurelike about volunteering is the unselfish regard for another or a set of others as expressed in particular acts or activities. The role of altruism is well understood in voluntary action research. Still, it is less well understood there that its expression is also highly rewarding, a sign of leisure in itself. According to the classification of rewards just discussed, altruistic action in career volunteering is a main form, if not the main form, of self-enrichment found in this kind of activity.

When Volunteering is not Leisure

Just as we can pursue leisure in both its serious and casual forms, so we can pursue volunteering. Some voluntary action is momentary; it requires little skill or knowledge, but is nonetheless satisfying, perhaps even enjoyable. Volunteering in an atmosphere of fun to take tickets or distribute flyers are among the examples mentioned earlier. Such activities can be called casual volunteering. By contrast, voluntarily giving blood or, in some instances, money (as a donation) are not really fun. But they can be satisfying, in which case they are truly leisure as well as fine examples of what Parker (1997) calls "altruistic volunteering."[2] When unsatisfying, when done as obligations, they not only fail to count as leisure, they even fail to meet our introductory conceptualization of volunteering. And let us not forget that, in anticipating a satisfying experience, some people volunteer to do something only to find it boring, difficult, distasteful, or in some other way disagreeable (e.g., Chambré, 1987, pp. 114-115). For the moment this voluntary action is anything but leisure. Moreover, the "volunteer" is now in the mood to abandon the activity at the first appropriate opportunity.

To this point, we have mostly considered formal volunteering. It appears to be somewhat more prevalent than informal volunteering, or "helping." Nevertheless, many people willingly lend a hand to a friend, relative, or neighbor to aid in a way he or she genuinely appreciates. This informal volunteering may well be leisure, either serious or casual, although this interpretation depends on the nature of the activity. Still, some people help their friends, relatives, or neighbors even though they (the helpers) prefer to be doing something else; in reality they are fulfilling an unsatisfying obligation. Obligated in this manner, these helpers are hardly taking their leisure, for the activity is neither truly satisfying nor freely chosen. They are neither willingly nor enthusiastically undertaking it to reach one or more of the rewards considered earlier.

Volunteer activity undertaken for occupational reasons raises some difficult definitional questions when viewed from the leisure perspective. A person who agrees to organize the annual company picnic, sit on a particular committee, or campaign throughout the office for a charity exemplifies one type of occupational volunteering. Whether activity of this sort is true volunteering and true leisure depends on how he or she defines it. It is logically impossible to label the activity either leisure or volunteering if, in the main, the person only agrees to do it under pressure from a superior. But where people cheerfully accept such responsibilities, finding significant satisfaction in executing them, then they have also found a happy mix of leisure and volunteering in a sphere of life where work usually dominates. Here personal interests and collective interests are joined in a common orientation.

Exploring a line of work by volunteering in it, a practice especially common among the young and the unemployed, constitutes another type of occupational volunteering,, which Parker (1997) has labelled "market volunteering." In this instance, by gratuitously offering their services, these volunteers hope to gain experience and eventually find paid employment (e.g., Mueller, 1975; Jenner, 1982; Ellis, 1993). Over forty-three percent of the respondents in the previously mentioned Canadian survey said they hoped to find paid work by volunteering (Ross, 1990, p. 27). Students required to perform a certain number of hours of community service as part of a training program are operating in a similar atmosphere of coercion. To the extent that any of these activities is accompanied by a sense of obligation and disagreeableness, it fits poorly the usual definitions of leisure and raises questions about its fit with the definitions of volunteering. It is perhaps here more than anywhere else that leisure and volunteering can diverge. Students and unemployed workers who volunteer for these reasons are not usually directly coerced by someone else to do so. Nonetheless, volunteer work appears to them to be a good way to put them on the inside track leading to acceptable employment in the future or successful completion of a program of studies in the present.

Because it is viewed as a replacement for work, the practice of volunteering chiefly for the sake of keeping busy can be classified as a third kind of occupational volunteering. Some of the elderly and the unemployed explain their volunteer work in these terms (Carp, 1968; Roadburg, 1985, pp. 107-08; Shamir, 1985, p. 341). Of note is the Voluntary Projects Programme in Britain, which is mandated to develop voluntary work opportunities for the employed and the unemployed (Glyptis, 1989, p. 68). Volunteers in this program see volunteering as a way to keep active and thereby maintain their sense of personal well-being. That it might be unsatisfying is no matter, for they expect to work as they always have, paid or not.

With respect to the volunteer activities discussed in this section, it is evident that, as their leisure component decreases and their coercive component increases, their fit with Van Til's definition of volunteering weakens in the same measure. Volunteering as a form of busy work for the elderly and the unemployed and as a job-finding strategy for the young and the unemployed can have a sense of being coerced, however indirect. Where a sense of coercion exists, it is more accurate to label this activity *marginal volunteering*, since it resembles work and other obligated regular activity at least as much as it resembles mainstream volunteering as examined in this article.

The possibility of coercion and marginal volunteering should make us cautious about lay usage of terms like "volunteer" and "volunteering" and what constitutes true exemplars of leisure and volunteering. For example, one reviewer of an earlier version of this chapter mentioned the recent trend in the United States for courts to order so-called volunteer community service for certain categories of criminals. It is hoped that ideas in this section have helped develop a critical conceptual eye capable of seeing the inherent coercion in such practices despite the language used. In any case, we shall return to this question in chapter 8.

Conclusion

Jone Pearce (1993, pp. 181-82) calls attention to a major problem that can arise from treating volunteering as a form of leisure activity, a problem that persists even after qualifying volunteering as special, altruistically motivated leisure:

> If volunteers expect their participation to be another hobby, they might reasonably be expected to treat it like any other leisure activity. Certainly, few people undertake hobbies that require the sustained discipline that usually characterizes organizational roles. Organizations which assume that volunteers are hobbyists must provide very short hours and be prepared for unreliable workers, or they must recruit only among the subculture of driven hobbyists. The practical difficulty created by this assumption is that what begin as a frank acknowledgement that the time volunteers will give is limited may be come a reluctance to give volunteers any responsibility at all.

Pearce goes on to note that, when activities such as volunteering fail to fall neatly into the seemingly appropriate commonsense categories - in this case "work" and "leisure" - everyone concerned becomes confused. Under these conditions, it is possible that employers will mistreat volunteers as well as underestimate their capabilities and contributions. In the same vein, some of the respondents in my study of the Franco-Calgarians (Stebbins, 1994b, p. 71) worried that linking leisure and volunteering could trivialize the latter.

The present discussion of volunteering and serious leisure suggests ways to counteract these concerns. As I have been arguing, duty and obligation find their way into all three forms of serious leisure, not just career volunteering. Moreover, I have said that a significant proportion of leisure volunteering is serious, not casual; it is career volunteering. Finally, the powerful rewards following from the pursuit of activities of this sort are likewise powerful motivators to return for more. Perhaps there is no better way to secure the faithful, punctual fulfilment of associated obligations than to organize volunteer activity so that it pays off in this profound manner.

In general, even while career volunteers are reaping a range of powerful personal rewards from their activities, they are making significant contributions to community and society such as by working in important public services or major public events (e.g., fairs, festivals, sports events). The larger collectivity benefits substantially from their application of assiduously acquired skills, knowledge, and experience while they benefit personally from the expressions of appreciation received from the recipients of the volunteered service. This broad, social utility of volunteers is also part of the serious leisure perspective as applied to them and their activities. But, in promoting the principle of leisure volunteering as an important personal and social resource, we must ensure that the connotation of frivolity so commonly associated with the word leisure does not subvert the thinking of either the people who volunteer or the people who employ them. The *serious* leisure designation may be advantageous here.

Hopefully the present statement will serve as a useful guide for research in this field. But what kind of research should we conduct? Research in other areas of serious leisure has been ethnographic for the most part, executed as detailed studies of particular activities (e.g., peace workers, stand-up comics, gun collectors, allotment gardeners, amateur archaeologists). Examined at close range like this, we can easily discover and most thoroughly explore the complex of costs and rewards unique to each volunteer activity, the careers available there, and the social worlds within which the participants strive to reach their altruistic and self-interested goals. To avoid accumulating a set of disconnected case studies, such research should be "concatenated" (Stebbins, 1992b). Whether done by individual researchers or research organizations or both, it should be organized so as to systematically explore a given kind of volunteer activity through a sequence of separate projects each built on the ones preceding it.

According to Jeremy Rifkin (1995), we are now in the early years of the Information Age, gripped by dramatic declines in employment and public sector service and a concomitant rise in the third sector and personal and collective dependency on volunteers. For this reason alone, we will need to explore more deeply than ever the motives encouraging vastly different demographic categories of people to take up this role. In this connection, it is now clear that each category is rather differently motivated. Moreover, it is clear that self-interestedness is common to all categories and that substantial measures of coercion sometimes obliterate for some people the leisure and volunteer components other people find there. Given the importance of self-interestedness in this critical area of life in contemporary industrial societies, we must devote more time to exploring empirically the complicated link between voluntary action, on the one hand, and serious leisure and career volunteering on the other.

Chapter 4

Casual Leisure

The term "casual leisure" is as old as its fraternal twin, the term "serious leisure," for the first came into this world in the same article (Stebbins, 1982) that contained the initial conceptual statement about the second. In that article and a number of later works, to further clarify the meaning of serious leisure, I frequently contrasted serious leisure with casual, or unserious, leisure, exemplifying the latter with activities like taking a nap or strolling in the park or, when pursued as diversions, watching television or reading a newspaper. Moreover, I occasionally added to these definitional statements the observation that casual leisure can also be understood as all leisure falling outside the realm of serious leisure. Over the years, other writers, perhaps inspired by my example, have also delineated serious leisure in these two ways.

Thus from 1982 to the present among those researchers who have written on serious leisure, casual leisure has been cast in a residual role. I am perhaps the most culpable in this regard, for I have used casual leisure, among other ways, as a foil to illuminate the distinguishing qualities of serious leisure (Stebbins, 1992a, pp. 6-7) and to describe its enthusiasts by showing how they are much more than mere dabblers, players, or dilettantes, all basically casual leisure participants. Looking back at them now, I can see that these brief, sketchy portrayals of casual leisure have been painted in depreciatory colors, which become ever more vivid when contrasted with the appreciatory portrayals of serious leisure (e.g., Stebbins, 1996b, 1996c), leisure activity commonly venerated for its worklike character.

Nevertheless, the place accorded casual leisure in the larger world of all leisure is, in significant part, a matter of personal perspective; researchers have different views of it and so do the people who participate in it. For the person presently studying or participating in serious leisure, it is the most important activity of the moment, an orientation that temporarily forces casual leisure to the sidelines. Yet, beyond the spheres of research and participation in serious leisure, it is evident that casual leisure is anything but marginal. Far more people participate in it than in serious leisure, and many of the interviewees in my studies of amateurs, hobbyists, and career volunteers have pointed out that they also enjoy and therefore value their casual leisure. In other words, casual leisure is an important form of leisure in itself and, for that reason alone, should be conceptually clarified and elaborated. And although such clarification and elaboration will also sharpen our understanding of serious leisure by further differentiating the two, the principal goal of this chapter is to present a theoretical statement centering on casual leisure as a field of its own demarcated by its own distinctive properties.

A Definition

Although there has been far more research conducted on the forms of casual leisure than on those of serious leisure, no one has ever worked up a definition of the former; hence no one has ever mounted a study specifically guided by such a definition. To fill this theoretical and empirical void, the present chapter sets out an initial statement, proceeding along lines similar to those of the initial conceptual statement on serious leisure to offer a tentative, relatively general, definition of casual leisure. A crisper, more focused definition should emerge in due course, one important result of future research on casual leisure expressly guided by the concept to be elaborated below. As a beginning, then, casual leisure can be defined as immediately, intrinsically rewarding, relatively short-lived pleasurable activity requiring little or no special training to enjoy it.[1] In broad, colloquial language, it could serve as the scientific term for the practice of doing what comes naturally.

This definition gives enough precision to focus inquiry on casual leisure, but not so much as to obviate changes to the definition that could emerge through exploration of its particular forms by means of open-ended investigation. In sociology, concepts of this sort have been described as "analytic" or "sensitizing" (Blumer, 1969, pp. 147-149; Glaser & Strauss, 1967, pp. 38-39). The following types of casual leisure should also be understood in these terms.

Types of Casual Leisure

Preliminary observation suggests that casual leisure comes in at least six types, treated here under the headings of play, relaxation, passive entertainment, active entertainment, sociable conversation, and sensory stimulation. Although the types are conceptually distinct, participants can and, it appears, frequently do, experience two or three of them while engaging in a particular leisure activity. No claim is made here that this set is exhaustive; research might well uncover additional types.

Play, Relaxation, and Entertainment

Kelly (1990, p. 28) has identified three central elements of play:

1. Play generally refers to the activity of children or to a "childlike" lightness of behavior in adults.
2. Play is expressive and intrinsic in motivation.
3. Play involves a nonserious suspension of consequences, a temporary creation of its own world of meaning which often is a shadow of the "real world."

It is obvious that some adult casual leisure activities can be considered play. It is less obvious, however, that, when they play, adults often dabble in or play around at an activity pursued as serious leisure by others. Examples of such lightheartedness are legion; they include the casual, or occasional, canoeist, tennis player, piano player, sport fisher, and stamp collector (the latter being more accurately viewed as a type of "accumulator," Olmsted, 1991). Some of the differences separating casual and serious leisure involvement in tourism and volunteering have also been examined (Stebbins, 1996a, 1996b). In general, in every serious leisure field studied so far by the author, its participants and devotees recognize the existence of dabblers there, oriented by a carefree attitude toward the activity that contrasts sharply with their own serious approach to it.

The *New Shorter Oxford English Dictionary* defines relaxation as a "release from mental or physical tension; especially by recreation or rest." We relax and thereby enjoy this type of casual leisure by sitting, strolling, napping, lying down, and the like. Also to be considered relaxation is the practice of idly driving around town or through the countryside for the purpose of savoring the passing sights. And, when motivated by the need for repose, boat, aircraft, and equestrian tours can be similarly classified.

In passive entertainment the diversion or amusement is delivered to its consumers, where the principal action required of them is to arrange for its delivery (e.g., by opening the book, turning on the television set, inserting a compact disc into the player). In truly, passively-consumed diversion, however, a film, live entertainment, television program, video or audio recording, or genre of written material (e.g., book, article, horoscope), there is, at most, only minimal analysis of or need to concentrate on its contents. People simply take in what they perceive, seeing it as something to be enjoyed for its own sake quite apart from any desire or obligation to study it in some way. When approached from the nonanalytic orientation of pure enjoyment, the category of passive entertainment subsumes an enormous variety of activities. But, to the extent that a person becomes actively involved with the activity, such as through analysis or concentration, he or she drifts toward the sphere of active entertainment.

In "active entertainment," as the term implies, the participant must act to ensure his or her own diversion. Relatively simple activities such as riddles, puzzles, party games, children's games, and games of chance number among the many examples of this type of casual leisure. But, when participation in active entertainment requires a significant level of skill, knowledge, or experience, it ceases to be casual leisure. Depending on the activity in question, it is now better described as a hobby or an amateur activity.

Sociable Conversation and Sensory Stimulation

According to Simmel (1949), the essence of sociable conversation lies in its playfulness, a quality enjoyed for its intrinsic value. Sociable conversation guarantees the participants maximization of such values as joy, relief, and vivacity; it is democratic activity in that the pleasure of one person is dependent on that of the other people in the exchange. Because it is a noninstrumental exchange between persons, sociable conversation is destroyed when someone introduces a wholly personal interest or goal and maintained when all participants exhibit amiability, cordiality, attractiveness, and proper breeding.

Sociable conversations can spring up in a wide variety of settings at any time during a person's waking hours. They often develop in such public conveyances as buses, taxis, and airplanes. Waiting rooms (e.g., emergency rooms, dentists' offices) and waiting areas (e.g., queues, bus stops) may beget sociable conversations among those with no choice but to be there. Still, possibly the most obvious as well as the most common occasion for sociable conversation springs not from adventitious events, such as those just described, but from planned ones such as receptions, private parties, and after-hours gatherings. Of course, to the extent that these get-togethers become instrumental, or problem-centered, as they can when work or some other obligation insinuates itself, their leisure character fades in proportion.

Turning to sensory stimulation, it is evident that human beings are aroused by a tremendous diversity of things and activities, among them *creature pleasures*, *displays of beauty*, *satisfying curiosity*, *thrills of movement*, and *thrills of deviant activity*. People relish their creature pleasures by engaging in activities where they have sex, eat, drink, touch, see, smell, hear, or feel coolness or warmth. Drug use intended to produce pleasant alterations of mood and perception as centered on such effects as vertigo, hallucinations, and mood elevation is another example of this type of casual leisure.

The displays of beauty may be natural, as found in water, clouds, mountains, or forests, or human made, as found in art, fireworks, architecture, or landscaped terrain. People satisfy their curiosity through casual leisure when they window shop, watch passers by, tour museums, and observe birds and animals (which might also be observed for their natural beauty), among many other ways. Finally, the thrills of movement encompass such breath-taking experiences as raft rides, "joyrides," carnival rides, and the bungee jump, while those of deviant activity are generated through such immoral pursuits as streaking, vandalism, and shoplifting (see later section on deviant leisure).

Combined Types

It is likely that people pursue the six types of casual leisure in combinations of two and three at least as often as they pursue them separately. For instance, every type can be relaxing, producing in this fashion play-relaxation, passive entertainment-relaxation, and so on. Various combinations of play and sensory stimulation are also possible, as in experimenting with drug use, sexual activity, and thrill seeking in movement. Additionally, sociable conversation accompanies some sessions of sensory stimulation (e.g., drug use, curiosity seeking, displays of beauty) as well as some sessions of relaxation and active and passive entertainment, although such conversation normally tends to be rather truncated in the latter two.

Hedonism and Other Rewards

This review of the types of casual leisure reveals that they share at least one central property: all are hedonic. More precisely, all produce a significant level of pleasure for those who participate in them. It follows that terms such as "pleasure" and "enjoyment" are the more appropriate descriptors of the rewards of casual leisure in contrast to terms such as "satisfaction" and "rewardingness," which best describe the rewards gained in serious leisure. At least the serious leisure participants interviewed by the author were inclined to describe their involvements as satisfying or rewarding rather than pleasurable or enjoyable.[2] Still, overlap exists, for both casual and serious leisure offer the hedonic reward of self-gratification (see reward number 5, chap. 1). The activity is fun to do, even if the fun component is considerably more prominent in casual when compared with serious leisure.

Moreover, my own observations of casual leisure suggest that hedonism, or self-gratification, although it is a principal reward here, must still share the stage with one or two other rewards. Thus, any type of casual leisure, like any type of serious leisure, can also help *re-create*, or regenerate, its participants following a lengthy stint of obligatory activity. Furthermore, some forms of casual and serious leisure offer the reward of *social attraction*, the appeal of being with other people while participating in a common activity. Nevertheless, even though some casual and serious leisure participants share certain rewards, research on this question will likely show that the former experience them in sharply different ways when compared with the latter. For example, the social attraction of belonging to a barbershop chorus or a company of actors with all its specialized shoptalk diverges considerably from that of belonging to a group of people playing a party game or taking a boat tour where such talk is highly unlikely to occur.

The fundamentally hedonic nature of casual leisure explains, in part, why this kind of leisure fails to produce a sense of optimal experience for its participants, at least when estimated according to the strictest application of Czikszentmihalyi's (1990, pp. 49-67) eight components of flow. Missing from the casual leisure activities, the enjoyment of which requires virtually no skill and only minimal knowledge, is the component of feeling competent to execute them. To generate flow, the activity must present a substantial challenge for those participating in it who, when in flow, feel competent to execute it.[3] Further, some casual leisure activities - e.g., games of chance, carnival rides, some sociable conversations - lack in significant degree the component of feeling in control over the way those activities are unfolding. Whatever a participant's level of competence, that person is unable to express it when lacking control in this sense. Thus, in the final analysis, so far as leisure in general is concerned, flow in its pure form is felt only in one sector of it, in certain serious leisure activities, an observation that squares with research by Csikszentmihalyi and LeFevre (1989) showing that flow and satisfaction are more likely to be found in work than in leisure.

Deviant Leisure

Most deviant leisure fits the description of tolerable deviance. Although its contravention of certain moral norms of a society is held by most of its members to be mildly threatening in most social situations, this form of deviance nevertheless fails to generate any significant or effective communal attempts to control it (Stebbins, 1996d, pp. 3-4). Tolerable deviance undertaken for pleasure - as casual leisure - encompasses a range of deviant sexual activities including cross-dressing, homosexuality, watching sex (e.g., striptease, pornographic films), and swinging and group sex. Heavy drinking and gambling, but not their more seriously regarded cousins alcoholism and compulsive gambling, are also tolerably deviant and hence forms of casual leisure as are the use of cannabis and the illicit, pleasurable, use of certain prescription drugs. Social nudism has also been analyzed within the tolerable deviance perspective (all these forms are examined in greater detail with an accent on their leisure qualities in Stebbins, 1996d, chaps. 3-7, 9).[4]

In the final analysis, deviant casual leisure roots in sensory stimulation and, in particular, the creature pleasures it produces. The majority of people in society tolerate most of these pleasures even if they would never think, or at least not dare, to enjoy themselves in these ways. In addition, they actively scorn a somewhat smaller number of intolerable forms of deviant casual leisure, demanding decisive police control of, for example, incest, vandalism, sexual assault, and what Jack Katz (1988, chap. 2) calls the "sneaky thrills" (certain incidents of theft, burglary, shoplifting, and joyriding). Sneaky thrills, however, are motivated not by the desire for creature pleasure but rather by the desire for a special kind of excitement: going against the grain of established social life.

Beyond the broad domains of tolerable and intolerable deviant casual leisure lies that of deviant *serious* leisure, composed primarily of aberrant religion, politics, and science. Deviant religion is manifested in the sects and cults of the typical modern society, while deviant politics is constituted of the radical fringes of its ideological left and right. Deviant science centers on the occult which, according to

Truzzi (1972), consists of five types: divination, witchcraft-Satanism, extrasensory perception, Eastern religious thought, and various residual occult phenomena revolving around UFOs, water witching, lake monsters, and the like (see Stebbins, 1996d, chap. 10 for further details). Thus deviant serious leisure, in the main, is pursued as a liberal arts hobby or as activity participation, or fields like witchcraft and divination, as both.

In whichever form of deviant serious leisure a person participates, he or she will find it necessary to make a significant effort to acquire its special belief system as well as to defend it against attack from mainstream science, religion, or politics. Moreover, here, the person will discover two additional rewards of considerable import: a special personal identity grounded, in part, in the unique genre of self-enrichment that invariably comes with inhabiting any marginal social world.

Conclusion: The Importance of Casual Leisure

The importance of casual leisure extends far beyond its theoretical function as the counterpart of serious leisure. First, it appears that very few people completely eschew casual leisure, whereas a great many people seem to do all they can to find it. So it is those who participate in serious leisure who are in the minority rather than their casual leisure cousins. And with good reason for, from time to time, people must rest, get away from it all, or recharge themselves to better execute life's many obligations. Furthermore, it was mentioned in the introduction that even serious leisure enthusiasts value their periods of casual leisure. Rojek's (1995) description of postmodern leisure as predominantly casual is consistent with this line of reasoning.

But - and this is the second point - it is certainly not valid to treat casual leisure as synonymous with mass or popular leisure, for many of the casual leisure activities in postmodern times are notable for generating their own highly specialized and exclusive "tribes." Maffesoli (1996) describes these tribes as fragmented groupings left over from the days of mass consumption, groupings with their own tastes and lifestyles. In this regard, they share some common ground with the groupings that have grown up around many of the serious leisure activities. Yet, even though it is true that the types and forms of casual and serious leisure vary widely as to the breadth of their appeal - many more people watch television than go in for bungee jumping or raising dogs - all tribalized leisure contributes in its own way to the structural and cultural organization of the community. Mass leisure, to the extent that it encompasses the leisure fads and fashions appealing to great, undifferentiated segments of the population, cannot, by definition, make such a contribution.

Third, playing and dabbling at an activity can give rise to new ideas (DeBono, 1967). Casual leisure appears to be the main source of serendipity in modern life, the quintessential form of informal experimentation, accidental discovery and spontaneous invention. This contrasts with exploration, which is a purposive, systematic, prearranged undertaking. In serious leisure amateur comics, artists, and scientists, for example, routinely explore, whereas in casual leisure players, sociable conversationalists, and seekers of sensory stimulation do not. Thus, whereas the first group occasionally discovers by serendipity, it is the second group who *only* discovers by this process and, for that reason alone, may do so with significantly greater frequency. Leisure, as Charles Brightbill (1961, pp. 177-178) once observed, is the institution in modern society most capable of engendering creativity and inventiveness. Research could well show that casual leisure is at least as creative and inventive as serious leisure.

Four, casual leisure has enormous economic import, since the bulk of the leisure industry caters to interests of this nature. The size of the industries serving such serious leisure fields as golf, tennis, sport fishing, and downhill skiing are hardly negligible. But they nonetheless pale into insignificance when compared with the size of those serving the vast casual leisure publics presently enamored of baseball, television, and social drinking, for instance.

In short, casual leisure also has its place in the sun. True, there is much to be gained from comparing it with serious leisure, and such comparisons should continue to be effected wherever appropriate. But to treat casual leisure as a residual whose only use is to further the definition of one aspect or another of serious leisure is to miss the opportunity to explore a leisure world rich in unique properties of its own. For example, the set of rewards motivating casual leisure - they are regeneration, social attraction, and self-enrichment - although it appears to be smaller than the set motivating serious leisure, is still well worth exploring for the similarities and differences separating the six types and their principal subtypes.

In this sense the present statement carries forward the theme of its predecessor on serious leisure published in 1982. The theme is that leisure is should also be viewed in another way, as other than a unitary phenomenon to be examined in great sweeping, generic analyses (e.g., research using undifferentiated lists of activities, theory purporting to explain all leisure), a dominant analytic and theoretic approach in leisure studies for many years (c.f., Hemingway, 1995, pp. 42-43; Roberts, 1994, p. 7). Rather, if we want to identify and understand their distinctive qualities, serious and casual leisure and their types and subtypes must be studied as separate albeit occasionally related sets of activities. This is the main reason for distinguishing these two broad forms of leisure in the first place.

Part II Elaborations and Extensions

Chapter 5

Cultural Tourism

At first blush, tourism and serious leisure would appear to go together about as well as pickles and ice cream, a seemingly incongruous, if not unappetizing, match on which most reasonable people would prefer to waste little of their precious thinking time. In common sense at least, tourism, according to the *New Shorter Oxford English Dictionary*, is "travelling for pleasure [and now] especially the business of attracting tourists and providing for their accommodation and entertainment." This hardly sounds like serious leisure. Viewed from the perspective of common sense, tourism, based as it often is on the pursuit of pure pleasure, is the opposite of serious leisure. In other words, commonsensically speaking, tourism is yet another form of casual leisure.

But as many a tourist researcher has observed in recent years, tourism is by no means all of a kind. As for common sense, Henry David Thoreau once noted that it "always takes a hasty and superficial view." In other words, from a scientific standpoint, certain kinds of tourism can be seen as far more than simple quests for pleasure and entertainment. This certainly holds for cultural tourism, which I will examine here, in general, as a hobby and, in particular, as a liberal arts hobby.

The intent of this chapter is to provide cultural tourism with a theoretical home, since it presently has no other. Furthermore, by integrating it into the theoretical perspective of serious leisure (Stebbins 1992a), we can enhance our understanding of its meaning for the tourist, its motivational foundation, and its place in the wider society. In harmony with that perspective, we will focus on tourism as seen and experienced by tourists themselves. Not under consideration here are the many related questions about their impact on the locality and facilities visited, the province of green tourism and the policy branch of cultural tourism.

Cultural Tourism

Cultural tourism is commonly contrasted with general, or mass, tourism, defined as "anyone who travels . . . such as [for] sightseeing, visiting friends, educational or cultural trips, participating as visitors at special events, shopping expeditions, rest and relaxation and others" (Kelly & Godbey, 1992, p. 405). After reviewing several recent definitions of cultural tourism, Reisinger (1994, p. 24) presents her own "broad" definition. It is paraphrased here as follows:

> Cultural tourism is a form of experiential tourism based on the search for and
> participation in new and deep cultural experiences of an aesthetic,
> intellectual, emotional, or psychological nature.

As a more concrete expression of this idea, she lists eight "purposes" for cultural travelling, purposes we can also use to distinguish cultural tourists from other kinds of tourists:

1) to attend cultural events
2) to experience the built heritage and natural environment
3) to demand experiential and participative activities
4) to seek authentic quality experiences
5) to seek individual involvement rather than organised mass tourism
6) to seek pleasure as well as education
7) to use travel as a means for personal growth
8) to meet local people

Tourists of every stripe have been described, among other ways, as people who are at leisure (Nash 1981, p. 462; Cohen, 1984, p. 375) and as people who constitute a special category of traveller (Cohen, 1974, pp. 530-531). But, to repeat, tourism and hence tourists are not all of a kind. Yiannakis and Gibson (1992, p. 291) in their synthesis of the existing types of tourists (e.g., Cohen, 1972) identified fourteen tourist roles only three of which - the "anthropologist,"the "archaeologist," and the "explorer" - fitted our conceptualization of cultural tourist. The anthropologists and archaeologists take arranged tours, the first because they enjoy meeting local people, trying their food, and speaking their language, the second because they enjoy viewing archaeological sites and ruins as part of their historical study of ancient civilizations. The explorers have interests similar to those of the anthropologists, but pursue them through trips they arrange on their own. Still, since they seek familiar accommodations and means of transportation, explorers rarely "go native."

Reisinger noted a critical weakness in the existing definitions of cultural tourism: the definition of culture varies substantially from one to another. However, the scant literature on the subject does mention repeatedly several distinctive forms of culture routinely attracting tourists, among them, museums, galleries, festivals, architecture, historic ruins, sporting events, artistic performances, and heritage sites. These forms serve as expressions or contain expressions of one or more fine, popular, or folk arts, or of one or more local lifestyles, which can be historical, contemporary, or folkloristic. Tourists make contact with such culture, either independently by personally organizing their own travels or collectively by paying an intermediary, an agent, to organize a cultural or an educational tour.

Given the aims of this chapter, it is unnecessary to go beyond the previously mentioned eight purposes to examine the several definitions of cultural tourism currently available. It will suffice to note that, when considered together, all eight find expression in these definitions, even though no single definition embraces the entire list. Note, too, that some of the definitions stress the profound and lasting effects of this form of tourism. As Delbaere (1994) puts it: "For us cultural tourism is a very broad idea which, beyond actual travel properly speaking, can have an enormous influence on the imagination, whether before, during, or after the trip" (translation). Such tourism, he adds, necessarily has a preparatory phase and it necessarily passes beyond the commercial husk of the site visited.

Delbaere (1994) also distinguishes cultural tourism from "recreational tourism," and we shall do the same here so as to clearly delineate the former. Motivationally speaking, the latter hinges on the tourist's desire to use a particular geographic area to express or realize an amateur or hobbyist interest. This interest is profound and, depending upon its nature, requires a certain level of skill, knowledge, conditioning, or experience. The modern world is replete with places renowned for such passions as golf, fishing, hunting, bird-watching, ocean surfing, alpine skiing, deep-sea diving, and mountain backpacking. In harmony with the serious leisure perspective, we shall treat recreational tourism here as either hobbyist or amateur activity carried out away from home by enthusiasts financially able to travel in pursuit of it. Thus hobbies (and amateur activities) pursued through recreational tourism differ from cultural tourism, a separate hobby in its own right.

Cultural Tourism

As near as I can tell, no one has attempted to link the concepts of cultural tourism and serious leisure as such. Yet, on at least three occasions, previous writers have, in their own fashion, seen a theoretical compatibility here. Krippendorf (1987: 134-135) describes the "new tourist" as a person "guided from within" who is ready to learn, sets his or her own travel limits, and travels by experimenting creatively. This profile squares theoretically with several of the aforementioned durable benefits.

Hall and Weiler (1992: 8-9) forged an even closer link with the serious leisure perspective when they demarcated "special interest tourism" according to five of the six distinguishing qualities and several of the durable benefits of serious leisure. They omitted only perseverance, a quality I will nevertheless reinstate in the Conclusion. Additionally, Hall (1992: 147-149), in a separate chapter on sport and tourism, distinguished between players of and activity participants in sport tourism, relegating to the realm of casual leisure those who simply travel to watch sporting events Gibson (1997) subsequently studied the demographic profile of the activity participants.[1]

But to argue, as Hall and Weiler seem to, that special interest tourism is wholly serious leisure and to refer to the former as a hobby, as the World Tourism

Organization (1985, p. 3) also does, masks some critical differences, among them Delbaere's distinction between cultural and recreational tourism. In other words, special interest tourism as defined by Hall and Weiler (1992, p. 5) is synonymous with active or experiential tourism, which is, in fact, a broad class of tourism subsuming not only cultural tourism, but also much more. The remainder of the present chapter shows, by treating it as a liberal arts hobby, when and how cultural tourism can be conceived of as serious leisure. As a consequence, it also shows when and how the other types of special interest tourism can be looked on as casual leisure (which is how Hall views spectator sport, for example).

A Liberal Arts Hobby

I am arguing here that the liberal arts hobby is the classificatory home of cultural tourism, which stands in contradistinction to that of recreational tourism. The latter, in harmony with Delbaere's definition, is expressed in the other types of hobbies, principally activity participation and sports and games, as well as in amateur sport.[2]

As indicated in chapter 1, reading, chiefly in books, magazines, and newspapers, is the principal way in which most hobbyists acquire their liberal arts knowledge. But reading can be substantially augmented by, among other ways, participating directly in activities related to the pastime. This is certainly true for the cultural tourist who, in fact, may consider reading and travelling as equally enjoyable and important, if he or she does not regard the first as augmenting the second. As for the travel itself, these tourists, as mentioned earlier, arrange their trips independently or, at times, collectively through an agent who organizes a group tour. The latter are not mass tourists, however, for, as Urry (1990, pp. 95-96) points out, the agent caters to small sets of clients here, treating each client with individual care and attention.

Some North American cultural tourists find an appealing balance of reading, lectures, and partly organized touring in the courses now available through a growing number of university noncredit, educational travel programs. The same may be said for the Elderhostel Program, which is composed of one- to two-week noncredit courses presently offered in over forty countries. It and the university educational travel programs exemplify well touristic, self-directed education in the liberal arts which, in the case of Elderhostel, is especially attractive for retired people. Additionally, several partly organized cultural tours as well as a variety of culturally-related camps and workshops are described in a recent book written by Fodor Travel Publications (1994). Many of the latter two, however, are most accurately classified as recreational tourism.

Still, some cultural tourism cannot be considered a hobby. Whether travel for the purposes of direct participation qualifies as a hobby, as serious leisure, depends in part on the pursuit of knowledge there being both systematic and enduring. A hobby is sustained over many years, not merely for two or three weeks of holiday time. From the participant's perspective, the vast majority of serious leisure pursuits unfold within the framework of a leisure role and its accompanying career as centered on the acquisition of skill, knowledge, or experience or a combination of these three. Such a career requires no small amount of time to take root and grow. An intense interest in an amateur, hobbyist, or volunteer activity motivates the enthusiast to use this time to pursue such leisure and the career it offers.

Consequently, people who participate in only one or two cultural tours, possibly separated by several years, who might nonetheless be classified in surveys as cultural tourists cannot, however, be classified in theory as hobbyists. Rather, such people are most accurately labelled *cultural dabblers*, which is a genre of casual leisure participant. In general, their participation in cultural tourism is so infrequent and sporadic as to render impossible its development as a hobby.

The reasons for this comparatively light rate of participation are undoubtedly legion and remain to be systematically explored. For instance, some cultural dabblers might find tourism of this kind to be less interesting or more socially or psychologically uncomfortable than they imagined (e.g., the food is too exotic, the locals are too different, the accommodations are too primitive). This is the outlook of Plog's (1991, pp. 62-64) "psychocentric." For some cultural dabblers, however, the prospect of cultural tourism as a hobby may be highly appealing but, unfortunately, too expensive.

At any rate, a proportion of all the people classifiable as active or experiential tourists who are participating in an activity for the first or second time (e.g., farm work, ethnic contact, adventure travel, or a visit to a museum or an arts festival) find this kind of touring sufficiently exciting and interesting to turn it into a hobby. The rest, for reasons like those just listed, fail to make this leisure commitment. They remain as cultural dabblers, experiencing the six qualities of serious leisure only weakly, at best, when compared with how much more richly they are experienced by the true hobby tourists (and, in their own fields, amateurs and volunteers). In short, being active and seeking participative experience (as escape, beauty, learning, emotion, novelty, enrichment, risk taking, etc.) are necessary but not sufficient conditions of cultural tourism.

The cultural dabbler is no hobbyist.[3] But the *cultural tourist* is, in part because he or she takes cultural tours regularly and frequently. Being active and seeking experience are regularized here, perhaps with a great deal of personal variation. From what has been said to this point, we can extract two types of cultural tourist. To the extent a person is blessed with sufficient time, money, and inclination, he or she can be both.

The *general* cultural tourist makes a hobby of visiting different geographic sites - countries, cities, regions - taking in a variety of distinctive, local cultural events and activities of the sort referred to earlier as cultural forms (e.g., museums, historical sites, arts festivals). The career of this hobbyist develops along the lines of accumulated knowledge and experience, which may get incorporated from time to time in an ever-expanding set of empirically-based generalizations about foreign culture. The participant arrives at these generalizations inductively by comparing over the years his or her experiences and perhaps those of others.

This growing "cultural" knowledge is augmented by a growing "practical" knowledge, including how to attend to everyday needs in unfamiliar settings and how to interact with local people. In this connection, cultural tourists in the role of explorer, anthropologist, or archaeologist are still cocooned to a significant degree in what Cohen calls an "environmental bubble," a set of accommodations and living habits sufficiently familiar to keep anxiety about the unfamiliar to a manageable level. He notes that, although "novelty and strangeness are essential elements in the tourist experience," they must nevertheless be largely unthreatening (Cohen 1972, p. 166). Both cultural and practical, the hobbyist knowledge base of this tourist is eclectic, typically including ideas about the local arts, folkways, lifestyles, and histories, occasionally broadened through comparison with geographic sites visited previously.

The general cultural tourist is possibly more prevalent than the *specialized* cultural tourist. The latter concentrates on one or a small number of geographic sites or cultural entities, which he or she accomplishes by repeatedly visiting a particular city, region, or country in search of a broad cultural understanding of the place or by going to different cities, regions, or countries in search of exemplars of, for instance, a type of art, history, festival, or museum. My enduring quest for an increasingly deeper understanding of Quebec and New Orleans puts me in the category of specialized cultural tourist. I have friends with a similar passion for France. Further, I know of people who travel far and wide to take in jazz festivals or theater productions and others who visit places expressly to tour the local galleries and museums housing such objects of fine art as paintings and sculptures.

Although their subjects of study differ, both general and specialized cultural tourists seek a kind of broad knowledge for its own sake. Such is the hallmark of the liberal arts hobbies. In other words, neither particularly wants a technical knowledge in this area as this idea was defined earlier. Moreover, by their very nature, both types are inclined to eschew much of the commercialized husk surrounding their subjects of study in favor of both savoring and understanding those subjects at significantly deeper levels of meaning. In MacCannell's (1976) words, they are searching for "authenticity." Commercialism is rampant nowadays, not the least in many museums of fine art where T-shirts and cheap mementos are vended in on-site gift shops.

Earlier, following Delbaere, we noted that cultural tourists prepare themselves for their travels. Although he failed to describe this preparation, it is reasonable to assume that he had intellectual preparation in mind. Intellectual preparation is primarily what participants receive in their courses in the Elderhostel and educational travel programs prior to embarking on their tours. But what about other cultural tourists, particularly those who are independent, who organize their own travels?

Little is known about how these tourists acquire the background knowledge needed for their next voyage. Perhaps they examine in advance the appropriate Frommer's or Fodor's guide or, somewhat better suited to their needs, the appropriate Michelin or Lonely Planet guide, which contains rather more cultural detail than the first two. Some cultural tourists explore their object of study by reading specialized books and articles in magazines and encyclopaedias. They may avail themselves of video cassettes or television documentaries on the subject, or they happen to know someone who has taken a similar trip and who is now willing to serve as a resource. Finally, people in the tourist's home community may offer the occasional public lecture or slide presentation bearing on his or her hobby.

The cultural tourists have only recently arrived on the scene of contemporary mass tourism.[4] If New Orleans is typical, we can say that cultural tourists everywhere are often forced to choose from two extreme types of literature about their object of study. At one extreme is the standard tourist guide of the Frommer-Fodor variety; it contains a great deal of practical information about the local weather, currency, restaurants, accommodations, sightseeing attractions, and so forth, but only a modicum of cultural information.[5] At the other extreme is the academic literature bearing on the object, much of which is written in language too obscure for the average cultural tourist and much of which is only available in specialized libraries. This was the gap I was trying to bridge when I wrote *The Connoisseur's New Orleans* (Stebbins, 1995), an educational travel book whose style is appropriate for both the general and the specialized cultural tourist and whose aim is to impart an appreciation of the cultural essence of that city.

It is in the area of background literature where specialized cultural tourists face a problem largely unknown to their generalized cousins. Having committed themselves to the study of one or two geographic areas or cultural forms, how then do they both maintain and expand their knowledge of them when not travelling? First of all, many of the means of preparation can also be used to advance knowledge between trips. In addition, the most enthusiastic hobbyists no doubt purchase educational material during their most recent visit as a way of tiding themselves over to the next one. Some of this material may only be available in the locality visited. Magazines, newsletters, and similar periodicals may also exist for some specialized cultural tourists, although a systematic study of these resources has never been undertaken. For example, *The Jazz Report*, a bimonthly magazine, informs its readers about jazz clubs and festivals around the world. Another periodical *The Strade* offers a similar service on a smaller scale for the travelling devotees of classical music.

Conclusions

To recapitulate, I have drawn on the serious leisure perspective to argue that cultural tourism (both general and specialized) is a liberal arts hobby and subtype of serious leisure. Further, I have distinguished it from other hobbyist activities and from amateurism, holding that, where tourism is undertaken as part of the latter two, it is normally of the recreational kind. Both types of cultural tourism were distinguished from cultural dabbling, a genre of casual leisure. Special interest tourism embraces not only these three, but also every other kind of tourism that can be actively approached through participative experience. Still, being active and seeking participative touristic experiences are only necessary rather than sufficient conditions of cultural tourism.

Earlier I observed that the pursuit of the liberal arts hobby of cultural tourism, like other forms of serious leisure, is driven by a set of powerful rewards. Still, with any form of serious leisure, its practitioners must always confront particular costs as well (e.g., confusion, social awkwardness, physical discomfort), even if they are invariably outweighed by these rewards. As for the rewards, certain ones stand out among cultural tourists: self-actualization, self-enrichment, self-expression, self-gratification, and enhancement of self-image (see also Hall & Weiler, 1992, pp. 8-9).

The last of these, says John Urry, is especially significant for tourists in the postmodern age. He writes that "identity is formed through consumption and play. It is argued that people's social identities are increasingly formed not through work, whether in the factory or the home, but through their patterns of consumption of goods, services and signs" (Urry, 1994, p. 235). In the postmodern age, Urry notes, tourism is a main pattern of consumption. Yet, if general, or mass, tourism is a source of distinctive self-identification, then the more exclusive, profound cultural tourism must surely be an identity source *extraodinaire*. Hall and Weiler (1992, p. 9) observe that much of \cultural tourism is undertaken with serious intent, giving rise to numerous special identities in the process.

Why should cultural tourism lead to an especially distinctive identity? Because it roots in the six distinguishing qualities separating it and the other forms of serious leisure from casual leisure, one variant of which is mass tourism. By way of illustration let us consider briefly two of these qualities: perseverance and personal effort. As an example of the first, I can report having watched people endure a most uncomfortable lengthy wait in the intense heat of New Orleans for the opportunity to sample Creole-Cajun food in restaurants renowned the world over for this cuisine. Effort in cultural tourism is evidenced, among other ways, in the extensive reading people do on the subject of their touristic interest. In short, even though some social scientists classify some cultural tourists (usually the anthropologists and archaeologists, Yiannakis & Gibson, 1992) as mass tourists, these tourists are still sufficiently individuated by their serious approach to tourism and their unusual tastes in touristic objects to stand out from the true mass of tourists now roaming the globe.

A distinctive self-image combines with the other rewards mentioned earlier to constitute a substantial constellation of motives for engaging in cultural tourism as a hobby. This conception, as we have already seen, raises many significant research questions. To terminate this chapter, I should like to put forward just two more. First, why, in general, do not more mass tourists take up this hobby and why, in particular, do all cultural dabblers eventually reject it? Second, how do cultural tourists discover and develop the study of their chosen cultural interests to the point where it can be described as a liberal arts hobby?

Chapter 6

Leisure and Selfishness

The moral import of leisure has occupied a significant place in philosophy since the time of Aristotle. Today Gerald S. Fain, in speaking for contemporary philosophy, writes that "to philosophers, leisure is a consideration for understanding the `good life' and the idea of happiness" (Fain, 1991, p. 14). More specifically, leisure can be viewed as an ethical issue. It can be judged "wrong" or "right," as Michael Litner (1991-92) demonstrates when he compares getting drunk at a party, driving home, and causing an automobile accident with simply getting drunk at the party and driving home without incident. In this respect, we saw earlier that society defines some kinds of casual leisure as deviant, for example, nudism, aberrant sex, property offenses of various kinds, and the excessive recreational albeit nonaddictive, infatuation with certain drugs and games of chance (see also Katz, 1988).

The central thread of selfishness is its exploitative unfairness - a kind of personal favoritism that infects our daily affairs. Yet, selfishness fails to qualify as deviance, as sociologists routinely use this term. As an act, selfishness falls on a different moral plan from, say, homocide, compulsive, gambling, or even nudism or marijuana smoking. It is, rather, a transgression of the folkways, or more to the point, of certain rules of etiquette and courtesy (cf., Cooley, 1922, p. 216).

Apropos the morality of leisure, it is well known in the common sense world that leisure is capable of evoking selfish actions. Still, it is by no means clear that selfishness is more prevalent in leisure than in other spheres of life, especially those of work and obligated nonwork. But in considering the sociological definition of selfishness presented in the next section, it will become evident that leisure certainly provides a rich terrain for this ethical problem to take root and grow in. Thus my goal here is to explore the relationship between leisure and selfishness, a relationship that has suffered from scholarly neglect to this point.

Selfishness

Downie and Telfer (1969, p. 39) note that "it is one of the most generally agreed upon judgments of ordinary morality that unselfishness is to be commended and selfishness condemned." That we condemn selfishness is patent; that it is inherently social is less so. Yet, its social character becomes evident when we define it sociologically as an act of a self-seeker judged as selfish by the victim of that act. When we define an act as selfish, we make an imputation. This imputation is most commonly hurled at perceived self—seekers by their victims, where the self-seekers are felt to demonstrate a concern for their own welfare or advantage at the expense of or in disregard for those victims (Stebbins, 1993b, p. 49). The central thread running in the fabric of selfishness is exploitative unfairness - a kind of personal favoritism infecting our everyday affairs. As annoying as a selfish act can be, however, it is probably most accurate to classify it as a breach of etiquette (Cooley, 1922, p. 216) rather than as an instance of deviance, which is a significantly weightier moral transgression.

A selfish act is goal-directed. Self-seekers have particular ends in mind, the pursuit of which results in what others define as unfair exploitation. Nevertheless, we shall see that the first may be surprised, even chagrined, to learn that their purposive behavior has been defined by its victims as self-centered.

The earlier definition, in its one-sentence simplicity, suggests that a victim loses something in this unpleasant exchange with a self-seeker. More precisely, victims impute selfishness where they fail to benefit as expected. A refusal to share a valued item is often at issue:

My sister got a book for Christmas that I wanted to read. She said I could do this after she had finished. Well, she finished reading it two days before I had to return to the university. I asked if I could take it back with me. My other sister would becoming to visit me the following week so that she could return it when she left. But my first sister was selfish; she wouldn't let me borrow the book for, at most, three weeks, even after she had already read it. When I asked why, she replied "because." That's selfish. Because of her selfish act ... I had to wait until next summer [to read the book] (taken from Stebbins, 1993b, p. 50).

The antithesis of selfishness, which is self-sacrifice, gives us further insight into its nature. In self-sacrifice one's person or interest is surrendered for others or for some ideal. It contains "breadth" and "magnanimity," as Cooley (1922, p. 220) put it, in contrast to the "narrowness" of the self-seeker's orientation.

This leads to a consideration of certain behavioral neighbors, or what selfishness is not. Nathaniel Branden's (1961, p. 57) belief that altruism is the logical opposite of selfishness (or egoism as he refers to it) is inaccurate. It overlooks the fact that we can be altruistic without engaging in self-sacrifice. Altruism is the uncalculated consideration of, regard for, or devotion to others' interests. A person might act altruistically in urging the government to tax the rich so it could help the poor. Were that person in the middle class, he or she would have surrendered little or nothing in making such an appeal.

Branden collaborated with Ayn Rand in *The Virture of Selfishness* to develop an ethical view of this attitude, one that diverges sharply from the conventional usage on which the present chapter concentrates. Their work is mentioned here simply to describe an established alternative conception, albeit one we shall avoid. Rand (1961, p. x) defines selfishness as "concern with one's own interest," which is virtuous because it is "rational self-interest" not one that is whimsical, emotional, or expressed at the expense, disregard, or disadvantage of others. Her "objectivist ethics" holds that actors must always be the beneficiary of their own actions. Exploiting others to reach this end is shortsighted, however; it fails to achieve happiness or even the actor's own values. Instead it transforms him or her into a parasite. Nevertheless, the commonsensical usage of "selfishness" fails to recognize such philosophic distinctions. And it is the commonsensical usage that intrigues the leisure studies specialist, for this is what he or she encounters in the study of leisure lifestyles.

Our conception of selfishness also differs from the rational pursuit of self-interest, which is occasionally cited as an important motive in economic activities (e.g., Parsons, 1940). In economic self-interest a person is concerned with his or her own material well-being and whatever advantage is needed to accomplish this. Obviously, some self-interest is also selfish, since it unfairly exploits others in certain ways. Under these conditions selfishness is but part of a broader, more complex transaction. Still, self-interest is sometimes pursued unselfishly. When a person's pursuit of his or her well-being exploits others, that action carries with it the possibility of the victim interpreting it as selfish. By contrast, an honest merchant seeking a fair profit, almost by definition, would be considered nonexploitative in the moral sense of the phrase "to exploit others."

Interpretation

The goal-oriented act of selfishness communicates a more consequential message to victims than self-seekers normally realize. A victim senses the strength of the self-seeker's aims and that person's desire to reach the goals even at the victim's expense. The latter also glimpses the self-seeker's image of him or her as someone who is powerless, inferior, blind to exploitation, unworthy of fair treatment, or some other humiliating imputation. Given this interpretation, the victim has good reason to define the situation as one of selfishness:

> An old boyfriend of mine was very selfish. When he wanted to see me he would phone and ask me to take the bus to his place. We lived very far apart, and he did have a car. He used to make sure I left his apartment for home in time to catch the last bus of the evening. He said he didn't want to pick me up because he shared the car with his roommates. My feelings were that he should have arranged to get the car when he wanted to see me (as he did to go downtown and the like). In my opinion the reason he didn't want to pick me up was so he would not have to fill the car with gas or drive to my house and back. I eventually stopped seeing him (taken from Stebbins, 1993b, p. 52).

The Ethics of Modern Leisure

When a strong desire burns to partake of it, any leisure activity is, in principle, capable of being interpreted as selfishly motivated. Yet, this tendency is usually more pronounced in serious leisure than in casual leisure. Ethically speaking, then, not all leisure activities come from the same cloth. Let us consider two ethical situations involving leisure, the first reported in a study of selfishness, the second in a study of amateur baseball players:[1]

> A former roommate of mine had a bad habit of monopolizing the couch in the living room. It was the only couch available and the most advantageous point from which to watch TV and stretch out, other than the floor. Although this selfish habit was somewhat trivial, I felt it a matter of courtesy to at least offer the couch to me occasionally. This never did occur, though there were times when its comfort would have been appreciated (Stebbins, 1993a, p. 53).

> Not hardly anything gets in the way of my baseball. I work my things around baseball. .Well, there have been a couple of times she [his wife] wanted to do things, and baseball got in the way and we did the baseball. But most of the time we got two cars, and if she doesn't want to go to my baseball game, 1 go where I'm going and she goes where she wants. But normally she ends up at the ball game sooner or later (Stebbins, 1979, p. 216).

The first situation exemplifies selfishness in casual leisure, whereas the second exemplifies it in serious leisure. Moreover, both situations illustrate how these two forms of leisure can generate their own distinctive moral dilemmas.

As mentioned earlier, it is true that, in principle, every leisure activity holds the possibility that, in one way or another, it can be undertaken selfishly. Furthermore, as the first problematic situation attests, those activities classified as casual leisure are clearly no exception. Attractive activity and selfishness appear to be natural partners. But selfishness enacted with reference to serious leisure interests is qualitatively different from selfish casual leisure in at least four ways.

One, when compared with the casual form, serious leisure is nearly always much more complicated and, for this reason, often takes up much more of the participant's time. Routine participation in a serious leisure career in theatre, mountain climbing, model railroad building, or volunteer work with the mentally handicapped is a much more detailed and socially complex undertaking than the routine pursuit of sun tanning, hot tubbing, weekend beer parties, or strolling in the park. The first commonly encourages expenditures of time so extensive that the close friends and relatives of the self-seeker sometimes see them as cutting into the time they hold to be rightfully theirs. These special others may lose some of their cherished benefits because certain significant people in their lives regularly and frequently devote themselves to a type of serious leisure.

Two, some types of serious leisure can only be pursued within a rigid schedule which, however, allows little room for compromise when compared with types that can be pursued at personally convenient times. Imputations of selfishness are considerably more likely to arise with regard to the first. Here, for instance, the participant may be required to attend weekly dance rehearsals, regular basketball practices, or Monday and Wednesday night meetings of two different volunteer organizations. People who can turn to their painting, stamp collecting, craft projects, or the reading of Shakespeare's works when no pressure exists to do something else are certainly less open to being charged by their spouses or partners with behaving selfishly.

Continuing in the same vein, differences in the amount and kind of selfishness even show up across the three types of serious leisure. Volunteering, with its roots in altruism, appears to be relatively free of selfish exploitation of the public being served. And it is possible that the altruistic attitude weakens or even eliminates the tendency to treat others selfishly while arranging to volunteer. But where this internal control is weaker, as in the self-interested pursuit of a hobby or an amateur activity, there appears to be, when compared with volunteering, more exploitation of such people as family, friends, and neighbours.

Three, we can make a similar observation about serious and casual leisure activities that exclude one's partner *vis-à-vis* those that include that person. Logically speaking, it is difficult to complain about alter's selfishness if ego also participates in the activity and finds it satisfying. I found considerable variation in serious leisure in this regard, with fields such as music and archaeology being found to be more amenable to family participation than those such as theatre and barbershop singing (Stebbins, 1992a, pp. 109-111). On the casual leisure side we can identify as inclusive family activities those of swimming, skating, picnicking, and dining out and as exclusive individual activities those of same-sex parties, meetings of exclusive organizations, and attendance at events aimed at either a male or a female clientele. Depending on how often people pursue exclusive activities, these activities are more likely than the inclusive activities to spawn charges of selfishness.

Four, serious leisure, when compared with casual leisure, is often more debatable as selfishness when seen from the standpoints of both the victim and the self-seeker. Serious leisure enthusiasts have at their fingertips as justifications for their actions such venerated ideals as self-enrichment, self-expression, self-actualization, service to others, contribution to group effort, development of a valued personal identity, and the regeneration of oneself after work. These ideals can be used to justify solitude, long hours away from home, expenditures of money, use of others' precious resources, and similar strategies, all of which can be enacted in ways simultaneously regarded as exploitative by victims.

It follows that amateur and hobbyist activities are especially likely to generate mutual selfishness, a situation in which each person in the confrontation views himself or herself as the victim and the other as the self-seeker (Stebbins, 1993, p. 55). My research on serious leisure suggests that its enthusiasts see their actions as serving in important and beneficial ways self, group, or society, if not all three, and claims that they undertake these actions purely for selfish reasons are themselves regarded as selfish. Confrontations based on charges of mutual selfishness often culminate in a standoff between the disputants.

We can interpret as mutual selfishness the acrimonious situation in which some of the female respondents interviewed in the study of barbershop singers sometimes find themselves. The singers said their husbands believed that their barbershop commitments encourage them to neglect them (the husbands) or their families or both. Yet the singers saw their husbands as selfish too. "He's not musical. He'll come to the shows alright, but I think he sees it as a duty. He complains a lot when I do work for the Board [of Directors of the Chapter] - 'the family needs you here, dinner is always so rushed on rehearsal nights.' You know, that kind of thing." (a singer of 12-years experience) (Stebbins, 1996a, p. 78).

From the various studies on serious leisure I have learned that the participants simultaneously regard the ideals they use to justify its pursuit as high-powered values, values quite capable of motivating them to continue their pursuits. Additionally, some of the values, for example, self-expression and self-enrichment, may also be endowed with a powerfully attractive autotelic sense of flow (Csikszentmihalyi, 1975). A person can experience it in casual leisure or serious leisure, although it appears to be more common in the latter.

Csikszentmihalyi identified several characteristics of this psychological process. In flow, performance merges the action of doing the leisure activity with one's awareness of it to form a unitary sensation. Further, performance centers attention exclusively on the limited stimulus field of the activity. When in flow the participant also loses his or her sense of ego, or self, by becoming enveloped in the process of carrying out the activity. A feeling of competence as a participant in that activity can develop from all this, a unique quality of serious leisure. Moreover, the participant's leisure goals at this point become increasingly focused, while feedback as to how well he or she is meeting these goals is immediately available in the unfolding of the activity itself. The flow experience impresses on the participant the autotelic nature of the leisure activity; this is an intensely rewarding activity in and of itself.

Conclusion

It is an ingrained rule of etiquette in Western society that we refrain from the exploitative unfairness of selfishness. Most people try to live by this rule, and most of them expect others to do the same. In everyday life, however, adhering to this rule can be problematic, for any attractive activity can lead its enthusiasts to depart from society's rules of etiquette for the sake of experiencing more of the powerful rewards that accompany it. Leisure in general is attractive enough to provoke the occasional breach of etiquette, while serious leisure in particular is even more likely to spawn this kind of misdemeanor. But ethical breaches of the selfish kind are sometimes difficult to clearly and convincingly define as such.

This is true because the fact of selfishness rests, at bottom, on the outcome of an interactive process, where the victim and the self-seeker negotiate whether the actions of the second are wrong, following the imputation by the first that the second is behaving selfishly (Stebbins, 1993, p. 54). But the imputation may not stick. That is, the self-seeker may successfully refute it claiming, as suggested earlier, that, for example, certain venerated principles justify the pursuit of the serious leisure in question. And situations arise where, although he or she feels exploited, the victim still remains unable to settle between the two of them that the other person is selfish and that exploitation has issued from this supposedly reprehensible act.

The point on which I wish to close this exploration is that, whereas leisure and selfishness seem to have a natural affinity, the link between the two is, in effect, a sociological contingency: Some self-seekers manage to talk their way out of the imputation that they have acted selfishly. In doing this they call into question whether the link really exists at all.

Chapter 7

Leisure Education

Charles Brightbill was one of the first scholars to acknowledge the importance of what he variously called "education for leisure" and "leisure education." He wrote that "when we speak . . . of education for leisure, we have in mind the process of helping *all* persons develop appreciations, interests, skills, and *opportunities* that will enable them to use their leisure in personally rewarding ways" (italics in original, Brightbill, 1961, p. 188). Given these words, I think it is safe to say that, were Brightbill writing today, he would argue that leisure education should center for the most part on serious leisure. In particular, such education should consist mainly of imparting knowledge about the nature of serious leisure, about its costs and rewards, and about participating in particular serious leisure activities. This conception of leisure education intentionally excludes casual leisure, on the grounds that such leisure requires little or no training or encouragement to engage in it and find enjoyment there.

Since the general public is largely unaware of the concept of serious leisure, the first goal of educators for leisure, who when conceived of broadly include counsellors, volunteers, and classroom instructors, is to inform their clients or students about its nature and value. Such information is important for anyone searching for an *optimal leisure lifestyle*: the pursuit of one or more substantial, absorbing leisure activities that together approach the person's ideal of a fulfilling existence during free time. More particularly, such education should be composed of instruction on the nature of serious leisure, the general rewards (and costs) of such activity, the possibility of finding a leisure career there, and the variety of social and psychological advantages that can accrue to the person who pursues it (e.g., special identity, routine, lifestyle, organizational belonging, central life interest, membership in a social world). In some instances, people will have to be told how to get started in the pursuits of interest to them. Elsewhere, I provide information on how to do this in North America (Stebbins, 1998a, chap. 6), which however, may sometimes be inappropriate for other parts of the world. Thus, to more effectively guide the people they are working with, leisure educators outside North America may have to gather information on how to get started that is specific to their country and local community.

In this chapter we examine two more elaborations and extensions of the serious leisure perspective, both of which fall under the rubric of leisure education. The first provides a link with the field of adult education, the second a link with that of disability research.

Adult Education

To my knowledge, the concepts and propositions linking the fields of leisure studies and adult education have never been systematically explored, even if the mutual affinity of the two has been recognized for some time and Faché (1998) has already linked serious leisure and adult education, albeit in a way different from what will be proposed here. For example, Godbey (1990, pp. 220-221), in writing from the leisure perspective, suggests that the greatest advances in adult education may well come in the area of education for leisure. Also of note is the fact that the World Leisure and Recreation Association included adult education in its International Charter for Leisure Education, a document ratified in 1993 (World Leisure and Recreation Association, 1994, sections I.4.3, III.1.3, III.3.1). Speaking for adult education, Selman, Cooke, Selman, and Dampier (1998, pp. 29-30) list four functions of adult education as seen by the individual participant in it, three of which - the social (roles in community), recreational, and self-developmental functions - bear directly on leisure, as conceived of in this chapter.[1] The social, or community, view of adult education is generally the same (for a review, see Selman et al., 1998, pp. 29-32; Jarvis, 1995, pp. 20-23). That is, through learning and in line with these functions, adult education is seen as contributing to the maintenance and development of the individual or the society or both. This, then, is "liberal adult education" (Duke, 1994), which is the focus of the present chapter.

The broad affinity between these two fields seems to be well-established. What remains to be done is to set out the detailed links that bind them. Five are examined in this chapter. The first link centers on the types of leisure that constitute the true focus of liberal adult education. That is, leisure is not all of a kind. For instance, we hardly need a course to inform us how to take an afternoon nap, stroll in the park, or gorge ourselves on beer and pretzels, activity defined earlier as casual leisure. In other words, we shall see that the leisure learned through adult education is usually of the serious variety. Second, people pursue such leisure in social and psychological conditions that are significantly different from the conditions in which they pursue casual leisure. Understanding these conditions can greatly expand our capacity to explain why people seek adult education as leisure and to describe the consequences of this activity for the community. Third, we shall further see that a number of serious leisure activities have traditionally been learned outside the framework of adult education, although it may be that organized adult education courses could serve these participants better. Fourth, at the practical level, people who learn their serious leisure by way of adult education find that this approach has both advantages and disadvantages. Fifth, at the conceptual level, the serious leisure perspective when linked with that of adult education adds significantly to the theoretical foundation of both fields.

As a guide for this chapter, we will use the definition of adult education prepared by UNESCO:

> Adult education is the entire body of organized educational processes, whatever the content, level and method, whether formal or otherwise, whether they prolong or replace initial education in schools, colleges and

universities as well as apprenticeship, whereby persons regarded as adult by the society to which they belong develop their abilities, enrich their knowledge, improve their technical or professional qualifications or turn them in a new direction and bring about changes in their attitudes or behavior in the twofold perspective of full personal development and participation in balanced and independent social, economic and cultural development (UNESCO, 1976, p. 2).

Learning - adult learning in particular - is the object of these educational processes. "Continuing education" often refers to the same processes, although the idea usually connotes furthering a person's education beyond initial education (Jarvis, 1995, p 29).

Learning Serious Leisure through Adult Education

Amateurs in the arts and sciences can avail themselves of adult education courses, and in the arts, even programs, that further their learning of serious leisure. The same can be said for most of the individual amateur sports (e.g., golf, tennis, racquetball). Still, if we examine the totality of adult educational programs in the typical North American city, it becomes clear that some amateur activities are ignored. Thus, would-be participants in such sports as handball, rodeo, weight lifting, and auto and motorcycle racing must usually learn on their own, by using books or by watching others play and asking them questions. Moreover, virtually all the entertainment arts must be learned this way. So far as I know, only Humber College in Toronto in Canada has developed an adult education course on stand-up comedy. The one-week "workshop" was offered for the first time in 1997 (Clark, 1997). There may also be isolated adult education courses of this sort in juggling, ventriloquism, and entertainment magic, for example, even though the general rule is that learning these arts is entirely self-directed, usually accomplished by reading, watching, questioning, and in some instances, finding private tutoring.

Adult education is, with the exception of collecting, a main avenue for learning hobbies. A great range of making and tinkering activities fill the multitude of North American adult education catalogs, including baking, decorating, do-it-yourself, raising and breeding, and various crafts (for a discussion of the many different hobbies, see Stebbins, 1998a, chap. 3). The same is true for activity participation, which includes such diverse enthusiasms as skin diving, cross-country skiing, mushroom gathering, and ballroom dancing. But here, too, activities exist whose devotees have no choice but to learn on their own, among them hiking, fishing (except fly casting), snowmobiling, barbershop singing, and dirt (trail) bike riding. Moreover, rare are adult education courses for the many would-be players of one of the hobbyist sports or games (those falling outside the category of amateur-professional sport). Most people in this area must direct their own learning of darts, horseshoes, ping pong, or handball, to name but a few. And those who go in for a particular table, board, card or electronic game usually learn it from other players or from printed instructions or from both. Still, adult education courses are readily available on bridge, orienteering, and the martial arts. Finally, the liberal arts hobbies are most often acquired purely through self-direction, chiefly by reading, as was noted earlier. But again we find exceptions, as in the general interest courses on certain arts, cultures, philosophies, and histories. Moreover, language instruction is one of the pillars of adult education.

Adult education courses related to volunteerism center mostly in such areas as fund raising and the management and recruitment of volunteers. To the extent that serious leisure volunteers are involved in these areas, they are likely to be interested in courses bearing on them. But many career volunteers devote themselves to other tasks, which they learn outside the framework of adult education. That is, the group (club, society, association, organization) in which they serve provides the basic instruction they need to learn further while on the job.

Consonant with Houle's (1961) distinction between learning- oriented and goal-oriented motives for pursuing adult education is the fact that the liberal arts hobbies are the only form of serious leisure where learning is an end in itself. By contrast, amateurs, volunteers, and other hobbyists learn as a means to particular leisure ends, such as producing art, playing sport, collecting objects, or helping others. Adult educators should not be surprised therefore if the latter seem restless, anxious to get on with what they consider the most important aspect of their serious leisure - *applying* what they have learned. Sometimes both types of participant enroll in the same course, a pattern that may be especially common in science. Thus, some of the students in an adult education astronomy course may be liberal arts hobbyists, while others are there to learn about the heavens as background for their research.

It is evident from the foregoing that liberal adult education presently provides instruction for only a proportion, albeit a sizable proportion, of all serious leisure participants. Perhaps this is as it should be, for it is certainly possible that the activities left to strictly personal learning are unteachable using the usual methods of adult education, or if they are teachable, that there may be too few students to fill the courses. Nonetheless, the discussion in this section contributes to the fields of adult education and leisure studies by identifying the many serious leisure activities not ordinarily learned through adult education (for a more complete list, see Stebbins, 1998a, chap. 3). By becoming aware of these activities, specialists in adult education put themselves in a position to weigh the pros and cons of teaching them. Knowledge of these activities can also sharpen our sense of the boundaries of this profession with reference to its social, recreational, and self-developmental functions.

Advantages and Disadvantages

The links between adult education and serious leisure explored in this chapter hold both advantages and disadvantages for serious leisure as an activity. At the same time, the links provide certain advantages for adult education and serious leisure as scientific specialities.

First, linking adult education and serious leisure serves to publicize the latter through widely-distributed listings in the periodic catalogs of the former. Such publicity is needed to help counteract the popular image that all leisure is essentially casual. Second, since adult education courses also work to bring people together, this link gives serious leisure participants an opportunity - possibility the only opportunity - to meet like-minded enthusiasts. We saw earlier that social attraction is one of the rewards of serious leisure. A third advantage is that, since adult education courses are taught by experts, they are routinely present in the classroom for consultation by their serious leisure students. Finally, organized instruction on the activity in question is likely to be reasonably systematic, or at least significantly more so than the typical program of self-instruction or on-the-job training.

Weighing against these advantages are certain disadvantages. For instance, Selman, et al. (1998, p. 353) point out that the expert-instructor may overemphasize his or her expertise and thereby undermine the students' autonomy. As students see it, the freedom to act is a cardinal value in both leisure and adult education. The authors also note that the course readings or a particular theory can blinker the students' outlooks on their leisure, thus threatening their autonomy in another way. Here students fail to take responsibility for their own decisions or fail to rely on or at least consider seriously their own judgments.

In the meantime, adult education can profit from its links with the field of serious leisure, possibly the most fruitful of which is the substantial theoretical tie set out earlier in this chapter. This is a tie with specificity, for casual leisure, which has no significant place in adult education, is omitted from it. The stereotype that all leisure is casual leisure has undoubtedly discouraged exploring how adult education and leisure studies are related. Moreover, that part of serious leisure theory centering on rewards and motivation helps explain in broad terms why adults pursue such leisure, and in the course of doing so, become motivated to learn it by way of adult education. This more inclusive motivational perspective is missing in the theory and research on liberal adult education, where emphasis has been more narrowly and directly focused on explaining either the motives for participating in adult education or the social and demographic context framing their emergence and expression (for a review, see Deshler, 1994).

Serious leisure research gains too in its liaison with adult education. For few leisure studies specialists have attempted to describe and explain how adults learn serious leisure pursuits (but see Carpenter, Patterson, & Pritchard, 1990, pp. 60-61).

However, in adult education, the field of andragogy, or "the science and art of helping adults learn" (Knowles, 1980, p. 43), offers a ready-made explanation of this process. Thus for adults, as compared with children, learning plays a significantly greater role in forming one's self-concept and is also more likely to be self-directed, by as much as 70 percent of all adult learning according to Brockett and Darkenwald (1987, p. 35). Adults also expect the material they learn to have a direct and immediate application in daily life.

Conclusions

Duke (1994, p. 92) writes that "over the past 40 years education for leisure, personal development, and self-expression has been a major growth area, especially among the more affluent middle classes of Western and Westernized societies." And there is reason to believe this trend will continue, for several writers, among them Rifkin (1995), Howard (1995), and Aronowitz and DiFazio (1994), have observed that the number of people with substantial amounts of free time on their hands is growing dramatically, parallelling the rapid spread of electronic technology across all sectors of the economy and the sharp reduction in employment opportunities that nearly always follows in its wake. One far-reaching consequence of this radical transformation of modern life, albeit a consequence these authors only allude to, is that, to find the equivalent respectable identity and central life interest they once knew in their work, more and more people will be forced to search for free-time activity of considerable substance.

In chapter 10, I argue that serious leisure can serve as the equivalent identity and central life interest (albeit a nonremunerative equivalent), that in the Information Age, this kind of leisure lies at the heart of a person's optimal leisure lifestyle. Liberal adult education, the present chapter suggests, has an important part to play in this dramatic transformation of work and leisure life. Indeed, without easy accessibility to such education, it is doubtful whether finding an optimal leisure lifestyle will be a reasonable possibility for many people.

Disabilities

Leisure studies specialists have all but ignored the leisure patterns and leisure needs of people with disabilities. As a result, says Prost (1992), we know little about the meaning of leisure among such people. McGill (1996, p. 8), makes a still more sweeping condemnation:

> Leisure as defined in human service terms, has not been recognized as a realm in which people with disabilities can explore or discover who they are and who they might become. There has been little recognition that supporting and allowing people with disabilities to experience the full range of leisure expressions is important to their finding meaning and creating balance in their lives.

Instead, she notes, leisure service professionals and even many family members concern themselves primarily with keeping such people busy. The thought that people with disabilities might take up a form of leisure capable of providing deep satisfaction through personal expression and a valued identity is simply incongruent with the view of them held by most professionals and family members (see Patterson, 1997, p. 24 for a review of the research supporting McGill's observation).

The stereotypes and flagging research interest notwithstanding, people with disabilities face still other problems. Prost (1992) goes on to note that many are chronically or sporadically unemployed, conditions so dispiriting that they are widely believed to stifle the pursuit of leisure of any kind, whatever the person's situation in life (e.g., Kay, 1990, 415; Haworth, 1986, 288). Furthermore, due mainly to the factor of unemployment, people with disabilities are commonly poor; this deprives them of the enjoyment of a number of leisure activities easily available to much of the rest of society. Finally, leisure is seen by many people as trivial and therefore hardly worth promoting for anyone, those with disabilities notwithstanding.

Nevertheless, a handful of scholars in the field of leisure studies have begun to entertain the idea that people with disabilities can benefit from participating in the more substantial forms of leisure - that is, serious leisure. Based on his research on people with spinal cord injuries, Kleiber (1996, p. 13) suggests that serious leisure activities could become an important element in the rehabilitation process of the disabled, possibly "by reconnecting with the self what was temporarily `lost' or in setting a new direction for a new self." Patterson (1997) forged an even more direct link between disability and serious leisure by explaining how the latter can serve as a nonpaying substitute for work for people whose disabilities force them into unemployment. In serious leisure, he observes, these people can find many of the same positive benefits they once found in their jobs:

> If people with disabilities are able to successfully participate in serious leisure pursuits, this can form the basis for self-respect and through their accomplishments something that can be viewed with great pride. Serious leisure activities create the situation where initiative, independence, and responsibility for one's own success or failure is the "modus operandi." Whether participating in a scientific project, an artistic performance, or an athletic contest the person is making a contribution to society that is appreciated by someone. (Patterson, 1997, p. 26)

The two main goals of this section are to inform leisure educators, broadly defined here as including leisure counsellors and leisure volunteers, about serious leisure and to suggest ways to apply it in the field of disabilities.

Leisure Education

As noted earlier leisure education should center on serious leisure, a conception that intentionally excludes casual leisure. Nonetheless, the preceding literature review indicates that, today, for most people with disabilities, leisure is predominantly casual.

Thus there should be two kinds of serious leisure education in this field. The first aims to educate or train people with disabilities to find satisfaction in an amateur, hobbyist, or career volunteer activity. This kind of education involves informing them in detail first about one or more of the activities which appeal to them and for which their disabilities do not disqualify them and then about how to participate in those activities. Thus one component of the job of leisure educator in the field of disabilities would be, for instance, to help people who are blind learn how to knit sweaters or play the piano, but not how to fish with flies or collect stamps.

This example indicates that particular disabilities are compatible with particular forms of serious leisure and incompatible with others. Rather than fill this chapter with lengthy lists of compatible activities for each disability, let me suggest that leisure educators present a list of all serious leisure activities (accompanied by descriptions where necessary) to the individuals with disabilities with whom they are working and then encourage them to select the two activities they find most appealing. The two can then be explored, after which each person can decide which one to pursue, unless he or she wants to pursue both of them simultaneously. This procedure has the advantage of avoiding the subtle influence of the stereotypes held by some of the non-disabled about what people with particular disabilities can and cannot do. As for the list, it could be developed from my discussion (Stebbins, 1998a) of over 300 serious leisure activities and types of activities and augmented with selections from the practical bibliography of books describing how to get started in them.

In this regard, the liberal arts hobbies are possibly the most appropriate type of serious leisure for the largest number of people with disabilities. For as long as the disability does not inhibit reading at a general level of comprehension - i.e., the person is not blind, mentally retarded, or handicapped by a reading disability - every liberal arts hobby should in principle be accessible for him or her. This having been said, we cannot ignore, however, the many leisure constraints that place some of these activities well beyond the reach of some people whose disabilities are not in themselves barriers. For example, Henderson and her colleagues (1995) found in their study of women with physical disabilities that, when it came to leisure, they were more often constrained by energy deficiency, dependency on others, and concern for physical and psychological safety than women without disabilities. In other words, to participate in one of the liberal arts hobbies, the enthusiast must be in a position to acquire reading material: have money to buy it, find someone who can get it, have it available in a language he or she can read, locate a quiet place where reading can be done, among other requirements. As a general rule, disabilities from the neck down should not, in themselves, disqualify a person from participating in most of the liberal arts hobbies.

The second kind of serious leisure education consists of instruction of a more general nature: informing people with disabilities about serious leisure as a kind of activity distinct from casual leisure. Here training is much the same for people with disabilities as for those without them. Since both the people with disabilities and the general public are largely unaware of the concept of serious leisure, the first educational goal here must be to inform everyone about its nature and value. As already indicated, such information is important for anyone searching for an optimal leisure lifestyle.

Two other dimensions should also be considered when discussing serious leisure with people who have disabilities: the time of onset of the disability and the prognosis for its rehabilitation. Thus, for each person being served, we should establish whether the disability was acquired after age 12 to 15 or at birth or in early childhood. And regardless of when it is acquired, we must know the prognosis for reasonable rehabilitation. Why age 12 to 15? Because by this age, some children have already developed considerable skill, knowledge, and experience in a serious leisure activity, most often an art, a sport, or one of the hobbies. Should they acquire a disability after this age and it fails to disqualify them from participating in this leisure, there appears to be little that leisure educators can or should try to do in such cases. Even where the disability does disqualify them, their earlier experience with a serious leisure activity could become a building block for educators working with the person to develop a new lifestyle based on a different physically or mentally compatible form of leisure. For the newly disabled person already understands the idea of serious leisure; he or she knows it can bring substantial rewards, offer an exciting social world and personal identity, and so on. Nonetheless, such people might still want to exam the broad list of activities to find the "best fit" for their personality and interests as seen in the light of their new condition.

A disability that holds out hope for a reasonably complete recovery in a relatively short period of time - say, three to five years - could differentially affect motivation to adopt a new leisure pursuit when compared with a disability predicted to last indefinitely, perhaps a lifetime. For example, a person disabled by a stroke who is told he or she will fully recover within four years may well be much less inclined to take up a new form of serious leisure than someone whose multiple sclerosis will, with growing certainty, permanently remove him or her from a sizable range of activities. Part of the educator's job in these instances, then, would be to learn the prognosis for rehabilitation of the people with whom he or she is working and adopt a pitch for engaging in serious leisure that harmonizes with the prognosis.

Conclusions

The two main goals of the preceding section were to inform leisure educators, including leisure counsellors and leisure volunteers, about serious leisure and to suggest ways to apply it in the field of disabilities. Taken separately, the educators, the counsellors, and the volunteers are trying to describe and explain to their target groups leisure as it relates to their distinct functions, and this chapter exhorts them to include serious leisure in the instruction they provide. Additionally, when compared with the educators performing their traditional role of classroom teaching, the counsellors and the volunteers are perhaps more likely to be involved in assisting actual participation in serious leisure. Such help is not unusual in itself, since people from all walks of life occasionally need guidance and encouragement in taking up and routinely pursuing a serious leisure activity. What is unusual, however, is that people with disabilities may more often need assistance of this sort than many other categories of people, if for no other reason than that some of the former lose (or fail to gain) the confidence they need to engage in complex, challenging activity of any kind (Niyazi, 1996).

Furthermore, counsellors and volunteers should work closely with individuals with particular disabilities to ensure on a practical level that they receive the training, equipment, and physical space needed to reasonably and effectively pursue their chosen leisure. This implies that, to provide this service, counsellors and volunteers working in this area should be acquainted with a wide range of serious leisure activities. It implies further that they should not only know how the activities are done and where neophytes can learn how to do them, but also what the distinctive costs and rewards enthusiasts in general and the disabled in particular are likely to experience. These workers do not, however, have to be able to do all these activities, clearly an impossible requirement in any case.

Judith McGill's (1996) pilot project shows the broad scope of the leisure educator's role is on this practical level. Herself a leisure consultant, McGill formed a committee from among the staff working at the Brampton Caledon Community Living Association located in Ontario, Canada, to work with and thereby help 11 people with disabilities. This was effected in two ways: developing, strengthening, or maintaining strong leisure roles and related identities of the 11 and, through memberships and social relationships in its clubs and associations, strengthening their sense of belonging to the local community. Reaching these goals required, in the first instance, getting to know the 11 people, which the staff accomplished by holding several informal conversations with each one. In these sessions, the staff learned about personal leisure preferences and "passionate" leisure involvements as well as about the meaning of and motivation behind each person's leisure and his or her patterns of participation in it. The staff and the 11 disabled people also explored the hopes and dreams of the latter and the barriers to fulfilling these dreams. Then a staff member worked with each person to develop a plan for circumventing the barriers, thus turning the dream into reality.

By no means all 11 subjects in McGill's pilot study wound up pursuing a serious leisure activity, in part because they were never informed about such leisure in the manner and detail recommended in this chapter. Nonetheless, her research does provide a variety of practical suggestions for helping people with disabilities develop, maintain, and strengthen their leisure roles and identities, which could be roles and identities founded on serious leisure were her approach used in conjunction with a list of its many activities. Perhaps the most important recommendation to emerge from McGill's research and from this chapter is that leisure educators must listen closely to the leisure hopes, fears, and desires of people with disabilities as they work with them to help them achieve an optimal leisure lifestyle as organized around a serious leisure pursuit.

Part III Research and Issues

Chapter 8

Recent Theory and Research

In at least one sense it would have been good to have blended the contents of this chapter into Part I, leading thereby to a convenient and compact statement of the serious leisure perspective as it has developed to date. Indeed, some recent recent research was incorporated in chapters 1 through 4. Nevertheless, adequate discussion of all the studies undertaken since 1991 in the name of serious leisure would have lengthened considerably each of these chapters, and in the process, detracted from the flow of the basic theoretical points presented there. Moreover, such an integration would have tended to minimize the contributions made to this field during the decade of the 1990s by an impressive number of scholars working in several different countries.

Still, a kind of integration can be achieved in this chapter, simply by following the same order in which the basic perspective was presented in Part I. Thus we start with some empirical and theoretical works that concerned with serious leisure in general and then proceed to those that are concerned first with amateurism, then with hobbyist activities, and finally with career volunteering. I will also follow in this chapter the internal order of chapters 2 through 4. To be considered for this review, each work discussed had to center partly or wholly on serious leisure or, in a few instances, provide rare ethnographic data on a serious leisure activity.

Serious Leisure

Several papers published since 1991 have come to my attention, each of which deals with a conceptual or a theoretical aspect of serious leisure. We turn first to Stan Parker's discussion of career.

Parker (1996) argues that the concept of career, on which I have relied so heavily in my studies of all three types of serious leisure participants, is essentially a middle-class idea. He theorizes that serious leisure, as expressed in five of its six distinctive qualities, is correlated with certain middle-class values, as measured by a list of ten such values developed earlier by Albert Cohen.[1] This is not, however, a one-to-one relationship. In support of this hypothesized correlation, Parker, Hamilton-Smith, and Davidson (1993), in a study of middle- and working-class men and women in Australia, found that the middle-class respondents were more likely to have serious leisure activities and interests than those from the working class. Parker (1996, p. 332) observes that "if serious leisure is to grow in the future, then it seems the middle class will be primarily responsible for that growth. Or perhaps I should say 'People with middle-class values will be responsible.'"

The findings from most of my own studies harmonize with the conclusions of Parker and his colleagues. Still, since there was a more even representation of these two classes among the amateurs in baseball and football, we should be on the lookout for serious leisure activities where the class ratio may be even or possibly reversed. It may turn out that these activities are mainly hobbies, among them pool, snowmobiling, snowboarding, dirt-bike racing, and the martial arts. Other hobbies like darts, hunting, and fishing may be found upon examination to attract a reasonably even mix of middle- and working-class enthusiasts.

Turning to another concept, Shamir (1992) found in three exploratory studies conducted in Israel that, on the one hand, the salience of a person's leisure identity is positively correlated with the level of effort and skill involved in a serious leisure activity. On the other hand, this salience is negatively correlated with the expectation of pleasure. His results help confirm several of the distinctive qualities of serious leisure, notably high identity with the activity, high levels of effort and perseverance in acquiring skill, and the enduring benefit of self-actualization. Shamir speculates that there may be a mutual cause-and-effect relationship between these qualities and the salience of a person's leisure identity.

Third, Goff, Fick, and Oppliger (1997) examined the moderating effect of spousal support on the relationship between serious leisure and the spouses' perception of leisure-family conflict. Their research on 580 American male and female runners revealed that, if they had spouses who ran, the spouses were more likely to support the respondents' running than if they had spouses who did not run. Family conflict is one possible cost of pursuing serious leisure, although I have found in my own studies, just as Goff and his colleagues found in theirs, that such conflict is less likely to occur when the couple shares the same leisure passion. Data from some, but not all, of the authors' measures also supported the proposition that commitment to running is positively related to leisure-family conflict.

Fourth, Fine and Holyfield (1996) explored the necessity for secrecy and trust of expert knowledge among a sample American mushroom collectors and mountain climbers. In the course of being socialized to their serious leisure group, new members learned early in their careers as hobbyists or amateurs that they can trust its experts, but must not make public the knowledge they gained from them. For example, secrecy prevents the public from learning about coveted terrain for mushrooming or favorite routes to difficult summits in alpinism.

Fifth, Yoder's study (1997) of tournament bass fishing in the United States showed, first, that fishers here are amateurs, not hobbyists, and second, that commodity producers serving both amateur and professional tournament fishers play a role significant enough to justify a modification in the original triangular professional-amateur-public (P-A-P) system of relationships first set out in Stebbins (1979). In other words, in the social world of these amateurs the "strangers" (Unruh, 1979) are a highly important group consisting, in the main, of national fishing organizations, tournament promoters, and manufacturers and distributors of sporting goods and services.[2] Significant numbers of amateurs make, sell, or advertise commodities for the sport. And the professional fishers are supported by the commodity agents by way of paid entry fees for tournaments, provision of boats and fishing tackle, and subsidies for living expenses. Top professionals are given a salary to promote fishing commodities. Yoder's (1997, p. 416) modification results in a more complicated triangular model (C-PC-AP) consisting of a system of relationships between commodity agents, professionals/commodity agents, and amateurs/publics.

The new C-PC-CP model sharpens our understanding of some other amateur fields as well. One of them is stand-up comedy, where the influence of a manager, booking agent, or comedy club owner can weigh heavily on the career of the performer (see Stebbins, 1990, chap. 7). It is likewise for certain types of entertainment magicians and the magic dealers and booking agents who inhabit their social world (Stebbins, 1993a). And Wilson (1995) describes a similar, "symbiotic" relationship between British marathon runners and the media. But, for amateurs in other fields of art, science, sport, and entertainment who are also linked to sets of strangers operating in their special social worlds, these strangers play a much more subdued role compared with the four fields just mentioned. Thus for many amateur activities, the simpler, P-A-P model still offers the most valid explanation of their social structure.

Finally, the extent of serious leisure marginality has come under some scrutiny. Taylor (1995) found that amateur archaeologists have gained a respected place in the vocabulary of their professional counterparts, contradicting thereby the evolutionary model that depicts the former as eventually being supplanted by the latter. And Baldwin and Norris's (1999) research on dog breeders and trainers in the American Kennel Club reveals that here, too, amateurs are also reasonably well-integrated with professionals. These two studies suggest that, while leisure marginality often exists in other parts of the amateur's life, in some instances it is significantly diluted when it comes to relations with professionals.

Amateurism

The research on amateurism conducted since 1991 has been confined to the fields of art and sport, particularly the latter. In the arts, amateurs and professionals in craft work and classical music have come in for considerable scrutiny.

Etheridge and Neapolitan (1985) studied a sample of craft artists in the United States. Their data showed that the amateurs were more serious about craft work than the dabblers, as measured by amount of training and propensity to read craft magazines.[3] Furthermore, the dabblers saw this leisure as recreation, as diversion from their daily routine, whereas the amateurs saw it as something more profound, as an expression of a strong commitment to perfection and artistic creativity. The latter, however, experienced significantly less pressure to produce for a commercial market than their professional counterparts. They also reported more intrinsic satisfaction with craft work than the professionals.

Juniu, Tedrick, and Boyd (1996) examined amateur and professional orchestral musicians in the United States. Not surprisingly, the amateurs defined rehearsals and performances as leisure, whereas the professionals defined them as work. Nevertheless, the authors found that the amateurs did not see the performances as "pure leisure" nor did the professionals see them as "pure work." In fact, the views of the two differed little in this regard. Rather, as argued in the serious leisure approach,

> a variety of rewards and thrills attract amateurs and professionals in their pursuits. In serious leisure and professional work, thrills are many; for example, just to be on stage and performing for an appreciative audience could be one of the main thrills that motivates the participant to stick with the pursuit. Thrills and rewards can be a powerful motivational foundation for work and leisure (Juniu et al., 1996, p. 55).

But in the rehearsals, the intrinsic motivation of the amateurs contrasted sharply with the extrinsic motivation of the professionals.

Although not specifically guided by the serious leisure perspective, Partington's study (1995, chap. 2) of Canadian professional orchestral musicians, nonetheless provides further evidence for some of the conditions that lead early amateurs to continue in their art, whether as amateurs or as professionals.[4] For example, he found that effort, interest, and background experiences were more important for a career in music than innate talent. Moreover, his respondents saw as crucial background factors informal opportunities at home, such as hearing music, singing it, and receiving encouragement from a caring adult. And memorable teachers influenced the musical lives of many of the respondents; they were described as role-models as well as able instructors.

Turning to sport, Thompson's research (1992) on older, amateur, female tennis players in Australia, though it, too, was not conducted explicitly from the serious leisure perspective, nonetheless provides considerable ethnographic data on a popular game whose leisure side has been neglected. Her study also contains data that support certain generalizations from my own research. Thus, Thompson's interviews revealed that, like the female barbershop singers I studied (Stebbins, 1996a), married female tennis players strive mightily to avoid inconveniencing their husbands, which they managed for the most part by avoiding weekend play. However, respondents whose husbands also played tennis escaped this problem, perhaps for reasons found in the Goff, et al. study (1997) presented earlier in this section. Although these women could play on weekends, they often wound up babysitting their children and missing their games when such a service became necessary because their husbands wanted to play at that time.

Yoder's article (1997) contains a detailed description of the social world of the American tournament bass fisher, where amateurs and professionals compete to catch the largest and heaviest fish within a specified period of time. In contrast with some national tournaments where prizes are as high as $100,000, local bass clubs put up little or no money, giving out only recognition for the top ranked fish. Of course, catching the fish is itself a flow experience par excellence, an intrinsic reward of considerable significance. Yoder found that many of the amateurs wanted to become professionals; this entails establishing a close relationship with one or more of the commodity producers in the sport, whose role there we just examined.

In what is quite possibly the first study of adult figure-skating as an amateur activity, McQuarrie and Jackson (1996) explore the constraints on a skater's progress through his or her serious leisure career in this activity. The authors found that, as they pass through the five stages of that career, adult amateur ice-skaters encounter and often successfully negotiate a variety of constraints. For example, many beginners, if they want to advance as skaters, face the problem of finding a "learn to skate" program for adults. Later, in the development stage of their careers, they must either compete or pass certain tests, so they can continue to participate. McQuarrie and Jackson found that the six distinctive qualities of serious leisure describe well the orientation and situation of these enthusiasts.

Hobbyist Activities

The most popular focus of serious leisure research since 1991 has been on the world of hobbies. This is perhaps as it should be, for the amateur field had been the center of scholarly attention up to that year, to the relative neglect of the other two main types. All five subtypes of hobbies have seen new work since 1991.

In the field of *collecting*, however, there is but one new contribution since 1991, a historical analysis of stamp collecting carried out by Steven Gelber (1992). He observes that this hobby emerged in parallel with industrial capitalism, the hobby getting its start in 1840 with the issuing in England of the first postage stamp. This was more than a coincidence: "I contend that stamp collectors transferred to the leisure sphere the discourse that defined the meaning of industrial capitalism and used the language and images of the marketplace to legitimize both work and leisure. By making their leisure like work, they could bring to it all the honor accorded productive activity in a work-oriented society" (Gelber, 1992, p. 743). The first stamp collectors were women and children whose interests in stamps were primarily aesthetic. Then, as more and more men entered the hobby, it became commoditized. They put aesthetic, historical, or educational value on stamps such that this kind of collecting could function as a metaphor for the free market: "a leisure-time activity that trained boys in the techniques and values of commerce and confirmed the legitimacy of the market economy for adult males" (Gelber, 1992, p. 749).

By contrast, the *making and tinkering* hobbies in recent years have attracted a great deal of attention. Let us start with the articles in this area contained in a special issue of *World Leisure & Recreation* devoted to serious leisure (Parker, 1993). In this issue (Crouch, 1993) and in a book published the following year (Crouch and Ward, 1994), we find both historical and contemporary analyses of allotment gardening as a form of serious leisure. This international hobby centers on the immense satisfaction derived from successfully growing one's own flowers, vegetables, or fruit shrubs or a combination of these on a small plot of rented land. Allotment gardeners are motivated not by subsistence needs but by, among other desiderata, a commitment to certain values (e.g., fresh produce, environmental conservation, closeness to the land); a desire to participate in the social world of allotment gardeners; and a drive to acquire and express particular skills, knowledge, and creativity. This hobby demands exceptional perseverance, a substantial asset in the struggle with pests, seasons, and disease.

Olmsted (1993) describes two hobbies in this category heretofore ignored in leisure studies: dollhouse building and model railroading. From interviews with Canadian and American hobbyists, he learned that both activities are highly satisfying, in part because they enable their participants to work alone. But they also have their social side, as seen in the small, formally- or informally-organized, local clubs, which meet regularly in the homes of members. Larger, community-wide clubs, which enroll many of the members of the small clubs, organize shows, hold workshops, circulate newsletters, and the like. Olmsted found that, since the media have little interest in these two hobbies, they remain largely unknown to the general public but, by the same token, they also escape being stereotyped by it. In this sense, they have avoided the kind of marginality that troubles much of serious leisure.

Another craft with no prior history of scientific study and one that knows no professional counterpart - only a commercial one - is quilting. King (1997) surveyed members of four local guilds in North Texas, where the level of commitment to and depth of knowledge of this hobby is significantly higher than among "casual" quilters (dabblers), who work alone at home. The hobbyists offered several reasons for quilting: it gives a sense of pride, it expresses one's creativity, and it provides an opportunity to meet like-minded participants. Some women quilted despite debilitating health problems such as arthritis and tendinitis. And even though quilting sometimes obtrudes on family life, as in travelling to quilt shows and festivals and spending money on books and supplies, the large majority of the respondents reported conditional or unconditional family support for their hobby. Nearly half the sample had entered their quilts or wall hangings in a juried show.

Do-it-yourself has also become the object of scholarly attention. For example, Chaplin (1999, pp. 48-49) describes the hobby of domestic reparations of British owners of second homes in France. In a historical analysis in the United States, Gelber (1997) observed that this hobby came into its own in the 1950s with the growth of suburbs and privately-owned homes, for apartment dwellers had no real right to tinker with someone else's property. Not unlike the context surrounding stamp collecting, do-it-yourself gained respectability in capitalist society because it had economic value, even though it was leisure, or self-directed activity that was at times even playful. It also justified the man of the house laying claim to his own special space: his workshop. But as Gelber (1997, p. 97) notes, "do-it-yourselfers in the 1950s seem to have been, for the most part, middle-aged, middle-income, white-collar workers, a pattern that remained unchanged in the subsequent thirty years." They could afford to hire someone to do their domestic jobs, but chose to do them themselves for the satisfaction of it all, a choice unavailable to the working classes, who presumably less often found leisure in carrying out the same tasks.

Moving to the realm of *activity participation*, Hamilton-Smith (1993) reports on the first exploration of "bushwalking," in other countries the Australian equivalent of hiking or backpacking. In Australia many of the participants in this hobby pursue it collectively through hiking clubs, doing so within a special cultural framework, or ethos, grounded in the belief in the rugged self-sufficient bushman and the desire for the enhanced social standing that emulating this type can bring the walker.

Nevertheless, the bushman type of hiker may be disappearing, increasingly displaced by commercialized leisure opportunities, where, for example, a professional guide assumes the roles of cook, map reader, and expert locator of good campsites.

The study of Canadian male and female barbershop singers conducted by the author (Stebbins, 1996a) stands as another addition to the activity participation literature. Personal enrichment was found to be the most powerful reward in barbershop singing. It comes through the experience of performing - mainly in presenting a polished show or selection of songs before an appreciative audience - wherein the performer is swallowed up in a sea of barbershop song. That is, when the experience is enriching, he or she is surrounded by pure, ringing, consonant harmonies (the hallmark of barbershop) to which the audience avidly responds. The study also examined the leisure careers and lifestyles of these singers, the history and social organization of their art, as well as some of the problems the art is facing today.

Sport and games constitute the arena of the greatest amount of research on serious leisure since 1991. Among the studies here is Apostle's (1992) fieldwork on Canadian curling, which is based on his considerable experience in the game. Although he describes the players as amateurs, the label of hobbyist seems more accurate at present, for making a living in Canada by curling is unrealistic, even if it is "virtually a full-time winter occupation for anyone who hopes to win [a Canadian national competition]." In other words, the most important rewards are still intrinsic: the satisfaction of playing the game and the honor of winning the major competitions. Apostle's observations belie the popular image of curling as a game of carefully-regulated emotion and hierarchical control of play by the team's leader, the "skip." During the matches he observed, there was considerable noise and loud communication, as well as numerous temperamental outbursts and unfriendly jibes at opposing teams. Moreover, democratic decision-making is considerably more common in today's matches than in the past.

Yair (1990; 1992) examined commitment among Israeli runners, who he classified in three categories: amateur, semiprofessional, and professional. The professionals, though they receive no money for running, were so labelled to reflect their high commitment to the sport, especially evident in the measure of willingness to endure the costs that accompany it. Thus, more than the semiprofessionals and even more than the amateurs, the professionals sacrifice time with family and friends and cut back on their commitment to their paying jobs so they can enter more races and train longer each week. Yair's research has led to a theoretical model of sport and leisure commitment based on four interdependent components: self-concept, activity level, achievement level, and commitment profile. Self-concept is strongly correlated with activity level, which strongly influences achievement level. Level of achievement affects self-concept and the commitment profile. High commitment is anchored partly in social structure and partly in personal circumstances.

Hastings and his colleagues (1995) have applied the serious leisure perspective to the careers of masters swimmers. Using data gathered in a comparative survey of Canadian and American swimmers, they concluded that, for both groups, the career contingencies of age, sex, marital status, and parental status influence the degree of importance these swimmers assign to their reasons for pursuing this kind of leisure. For example, males assign a lower importance to the reward of enjoyment of swimming than females do. Similarly, younger swimmers give a lower priority to enjoyment than older ones, as do Canadians when compared with Americans. Masters swimmers were more likely than those who had never competed at this level to value swimming for such reasons as achievement and skill development rather than enjoyment.

Subsequently, Hastings, Kurth, and Schloder (1996) turned to the work routines of these swimmers, which they view as an integral part of their leisure career since they spend so much more time here than in formal competitions. In sport and the arts, serious leisure work routines are overseen some of the time by a recognized expert (e.g., coach, teacher, director). The routines of masters swimming were found to consist of three dimensions, which the authors believe can also be found in the equivalent routines in the arts. The cognitive dimension refers to the scientific paradigms that explain how activities and performances occur as well as to the exemplars of these two. The logistical dimension centers on the availability of the resources needed to engage in the activity, including props, coaches, costumes, directors, swimming pools, and rehearsal space. The social dimension is composed of various social, personal, and organizational links, exemplified in the intersection of personal timetables and organized rehearsal and practice schedules. Among the many findings in this study is the observation concerning the cognitive dimension: forty years ago the training of swimmers was not organized in phases as it is today. In contrast, the modern swimmer is brought to his or her performance peak for a particular meet through a stepwise progression of coaching and training.

So far, contract bridge is the only game to have been examined under the banner of serious leisure. Scott and Godbey (1992) provide an ethnography of its social world, a world differentiated according to those who approach the game as a social activity and those who approach it as a serious activity. The authors studied bridge clubs in the United States, where those composed of women and those composed of couples could be described according to one of these two orientations. The typical social bridge club recruits by invitation and personal compatibility with its members. Its primary function is to strengthen interpersonal ties within the club, which meets in the players' homes. When together, members chat about work, friends, and family. On the other hand, the typical serious club, given its primary function of providing opportunities to play bridge, recruits openly according to ability. Games commonly take place at the club's facility, where talk tends to center on bridge strategy and bridge stories. The serious clubs are members of the American Contract Bridge League; the social clubs are not.

Scott and Godbey (1994) then proceeded to explore the question of recreational specialization in the social world of bridge. They identified four types of players within the subworlds of social and serious bridge: tournament, regular duplicate, regular social, and occasional. The first two types, who the authors saw as serious leisure participants, inhabit the social world of serious bridge, whereas the second two, who they viewed as casual leisure participants, are found in the world of social bridge.

Ronald Lambert (1995a, 1995b, 1996a, 1996b) has executed a rare study in the field of the *liberal arts hobbies*, in this instance family history.[5] Based on data gathered in Ontario, Canada, he found that genealogists there were primarily motivated to pursue this form of serious leisure by a passion to know their ancestors as people, learn about their own family roots, and be able to pass on this knowledge to future generations. Lambert learned that the most common sources of interest in becoming a family historian are family stories, examples of other family members doing genealogies, and requests for information about ancestors. The deaths of close family members and the presence of family artefacts also encouraged people to take up this hobby. The role of family historian, it turns out, is highly valued by those who fill it, for it gives focus to their lives and provides a sense of self-worth, a form of intellectual and emotional stimulation, a valued position within the family, and a perspective on time that unites past, present, and future. Some respondents said that the role also compensated for deficiencies in their work lives.

So far, the only other examination of this type of hobby is my own on cultural tourism, which however, centers on a particular tourist attraction - New Orleans - rather than on the tourists who go there (Stebbins, 1995). The study identifies and examines the five "cultural areas" that distinguish this city: jazz, lifestyle, history, architecture, and Creole-Cajun cuisine. They are the objects of scrutiny of those liberal arts hobbyists who specialize in urban cultural tourism. And throughout, the study juxtaposes commercial and authentic culture, exemplifying thus the challenges cultural tourists face as they work to separate the two.

Career Volunteering

Of the three main types, the concepts and propositions composing the career volunteering part of the serious leisure perspective have the least empirical support. Nevertheless, there has been some research, even if it is of very recent origin. In fact, we already encountered some of it in chapter 3, where I reported a few of the generalizations about the rewards experienced in career volunteering made in studies by Arai and Pedlar (1997) and myself (Stebbins, 1998b).

My own study of francophone volunteers in urban Alberta in Canada (Stebbins, 1998b) concentrated on the careers, costs and rewards, lifestyles, and community contributions of "key" volunteers. A key volunteer is a highly committed community servant, working in one or two enduring, official, responsible posts within one or more grassroots groups or organizations.[6] One section of the study dealt with two questions, both being sources of considerable confusion in the field of research on voluntary action and citizen participation: whether volunteering is done by choice or by obligation and whether it is done as work or as leisure. The study revealed that most of the Alberta key volunteers feel a general obligation to volunteer in their local francophone community, but that they also feel they can choose the particular posts they will work in and how long they stay in them. It further revealed that they had no trouble defining their volunteering as serious leisure once this leisure was described to them, but that without this information they tended to define it as work or as activity that is neither work nor leisure. As is typical in the commonsense world, nearly all the respondents looked on leisure as casual leisure, a conception that clashed head-on with the way they viewed their volunteering in the local francophone community.

Thompson (1997a) studied volunteer firefighters, who also work in the Province of Alberta. She observed the anomaly that, at the organizational level, volunteer fire departments operate like independent nonprofit organizations, even though they are actually units of local government. After examining the possibility that these firefighters might be described as amateurs, Thompson concluded that "volunteer" is still the best adjective, for they and their counterparts for whom firefighting is a livelihood do basically the same kind of work and it is doubtful that occupational firefighting constitutes a profession, sociologically speaking. Whichever their classification, these men and women find an appealing local identity in their serious leisure, a rich social world in which to participate, and a vigorous central life interest to absorb their free time.

Additionally, a set of articles on volunteering, with nearly every one centered on career volunteering, appeared in a special issue of *World Leisure & Recreation* (Stebbins, 1997c), which was published to commemorate the new Volunteerism Commission of the World Leisure and Recreation Association.[7] In their article, Jarvis and King (1997) discuss their study of volunteers working in a sample of Scout and Guide organizations in England. They found that one main reason for volunteering in these two organizations was for the enjoyment gained from working with children and youth. Their respondents gave work or family commitments as the two principal reasons for leaving the Guides and Scouts. Additionally, Nichols and King (1999) found that Guiding conformed to the six characteristics of serious leisure, as presented in chapter 1.

The same issue contains a report on an Australian survey conducted by Cuskelly and Harrington (1997), the results of which are organized along their work/leisure continuum of typologies of volunteering in sport. They first classified their respondents as either marginal or career volunteers, after which the former were further classified as "obligeers" or "role dependees" and the latter further classified as "altruistic leisure careerists" or "self-interested leisure careerists." Their data revealed that the marginal volunteers fall toward the leisure pole of the continuum, while the career volunteers fall toward the work pole, in that the second see their volunteering as serious leisure, activity that resembles work in certain ways.

Arai (1997) observed in her study that voluntary action and the environment in which it is carried out are presently undergoing momentous change and that empowerment theory can help us understand this change as it bears on volunteers and volunteering. To this end, Arai explored the relationship between empowerment, volunteering, and serious leisure, examining not only the benefits of these two pursuits for self and community, but also their undesirable, or "dark," side. She concludes that, whereas volunteering often takes the form of serious leisure, we must nevertheless be sure to examine the negative implications of this kind of activity, which include certain tensions and power relationships that emerge at both the personal and the community levels.

Benoit and Perkins (1997) combine the concepts of serious leisure and expressive and instrumental activity in their description and explanation of volunteer firefighting in Canada and the United States. Drawing mainly on their own research in this field, they conceive of the firefighter's role as a combination of serious leisure that is expressive activity and work that is distasteful, or instrumental activity, which is nevertheless frequently embellished with expressive actions. These three concepts then become the basis for generating some policy suggestions aimed at encouraging fund-raising to benefit not only the local volunteer fire department but also the community it serves.

Thompson (1997b) examines employment-based volunteering, in particular the situation in which a person who is employed by a profit-making corporation performs labor for a community charitable organization during periods of time normally dedicated to employment tasks. This is done, however, as part of an organized corporate program in which the employer actively and routinely encourages this sort of involvement. Thompson provides a complicated answer to the question of when employment-based volunteering is leisure and when it is not. She concludes that such volunteering is marginal leisure when compared with many other types of leisure.

Mixed Serious Leisure

Hamilton-Smith (1993, p. 12) noted in the course of relating Myles Dunphy's bushwalking career that "serious leisure may involve a multiplicity of possible roles: amateur, hobbyist, volunteer, activist, organiser, and certainly others." Dunphy himself played many of these roles. Moreover, his career evolved over the years as he adopted new leisure roles, while spending less time in some of the older ones. My own research corroborates these observations, suggesting further that possibly the most common change is for the participant to add a volunteer component to his or her amateur or hobbyist activity, as in becoming president of the community orchestra or treasurer of the local model railroad club.

Indeed, there is at least one field where mixed serious leisure appears to be the norm: historical reenactment. Mittelstaedt (1995) observed in his study of Americans reenacting the Civil War that they are first of all amateur historians. However, when he or she presents "living history" before an audience, each historian must also become an amateur actor. And to ensure realism, some of these enthusiasts go still further to become makers of such items as horseshoes and laundry soap that were in use at the time but cannot be found today in the same form (Mittelstaedt, 1990-91). A similar multiplicity of roles is evident in Revolutionary War reenactments (McKim, 1997) and, I should imagine, in the activities of the Society of Creative Anachronism, an international organization dedicated to researching and recreating pre-seventeenth century European history.

Conclusions

There can be no doubt that the serious leisure perspective has generated a remarkable amount of theory and research in the seven years between 1991 and early 1998, the time at which this chapter is being written. Not counting my own, there are possibly three to four times as many publications on the subject as in the 12-year period running from 1979 (the year *Amateurs* was published) to 1991. If one measure of the goodness of a scientific perspective is its intellectual fecundity, then the fertility rate of the serious leisure perspective stands as reasonable evidence of this attribute.

Nonetheless, it is also evident that its progeny have been enormously varied, for the researchers and theorists involved have employed the perspective in many different ways. Some have used it to shed light on research questions brought in from other areas of leisure studies. Most, however, have selected an aspect of the perspective and studied it further, or they have explored a form of serious leisure that had not yet been scientifically examined. I think *some* coordination of efforts in this regard would be good, and I once tried to start an institute fired by just such a mission. (It is perhaps no surprise that official enthusiasm for this project was conspicuously absent.) But I underscore the adjective "some" because I believe that individual selection of empirical and theoretical questions within the perspective is also good, for the perspective needs to be further tested and explored from every conceivable angle. We are highly unlikely to find this breadth of vision in any one institute director or coordinating committee.

This having been said, the next chapter looks at some of the current theoretical issues in the field. In themselves, they set a research agenda.

Chapter 9

Current Issues

Over the years in the field of leisure studies as well as in the preceding chapters of this book, there has been sporadic discussion of various conceptual and practical issues related to serious leisure. I examine these issues in this chapter, suggesting solutions wherever possible. The issues to be treated are career, well-being, unemployment, retirement, and serious leisure outside the First World.

Career

It was stated in chapter 1 that amateurs, hobbyists, and volunteers find careers in these roles and that this experience serves as one of six distinguishing qualities of serious leisure. Parker (1996, pp. 327-328), however, has two reservations about employing the concept of career in leisure studies:

> Let us turn to the first reservation. One is that "career" is essentially a *work* term. There is no reason why it should not be imported into fields other than work (we hear, sometimes, talk of a delinquency career, for example, but we should be aware of the dangers of conceptualising leisure in work terms rather than in its own (leisure) terms. . . . My second point is that "career" is essentially a middle-class concept. . . . People who would generally be regarded as middle class talk a lot about "career" and their own work histories usually follow Stebbins' five stages of progression. Working-class people, however, don't have careers - they simply have jobs, if they are lucky enough to get them.

As Parker notes the idea of career can be been imported into fields quite distant from the study of work, and a justification for doing so is found in the opening paragraph of chapter 1. Moreover, it is not at all evident that using this alien idea in leisure studies has caused any noticeable harm. Rather career has been used to good effect in serious leisure research for some time by me and more recently by others (see Scott & Godbey, 1994, p. 293; Hastings, et al., 1995; Hastings, et al., 1996; McQuarrie & Jackson, 1996). Additionally, the fact that amateurs, hobbyists, and volunteers have careers, helps drive home the important point that, in certain ways, serious leisure *is* like work. Nevertheless, serious leisure is "on the margin" between work and casual leisure (where there is no career). Therefore, we should expect research on serious leisure careers to reveal that, when compared with work careers, they have different content and different patterns of choice and obligation.

I addressed myself to Parker's second reservation in the preceding chapter, where I indicated that most of my own studies harmonize with his observations about the middle-class basis of serious leisure. But I also listed there several sports holding substantial appeal for the working classes. Now I would like to add that, should these people as workers fail to find a career in their work, they will surely find one in their serious leisure, provided they discover an attractive form of it and stay with it. That career could be in darts, dirt-bike racing, tournament bass fishing, or a number of other fields. But, to repeat, the career they find will be a leisure career characterized by its own distinctive qualities.

Parker (1996, p. 332) concludes his discussion with the following observation: "I disagree with Stebbins' claim that career is a defining characteristic of serious leisure because I think it is possible to be a good amateur, hobbyist, or volunteer with little or no thought of career." I can agree with this proposition, if it refers strictly to neophyte participants, who have yet to discover the career-like features of serious leisure. I have no doubt that many people taking up serious leisure for the first time give little or no thought to finding a career in it. But once neophytes begin to develop skills, knowledge, and sophistication in their activity, once they experience major accomplishments there, once they know what they can become from observing local devotees, then my research shows that they also begin to acquire a sense of career, albeit a "subjective" sense of it (Stebbins, 1970). In other words, the sense of career in leisure comes largely from monitoring and interpreting one's own personal growth and development, unlike many work careers the sense of which is substantially rooted in climbing an organizational hierarchy.

Well-Being

Research on well-being got its start in the study of work, or more accurately, in the study of its absence as experienced in unemployment. Jahoda (1979) set the stage for an extensive program of research in social psychology when she hypothesized that employment provides five categories of experience that are vital for well-being: time structure, social contacts, collective purpose, sense of identity, and regular activity. Since then, several investigators have shown that Jahoda's position was too one-sided (for a review see Haworth, 1997, chap. 3), that leisure can also contribute to well-being, even if their findings suggest that, in certain unemployment situations, its effect is muted. And among those concerned with the leisure-in-unemployment issue, a few, including me, have suggested that serious leisure might be the best kind of leisure for overcoming the dreary effects of the lack of work, while contributing significantly to personal well-being in the process (see also Samuel, 1994b, p. 6; Haworth, 1994, p. 13).

The first question to pose in this regard is whether a serious leisure activity, though freely chosen, can engender well-being when encumbered with significant costs and a marginal status *vis-à-vis* three major social institutions, namely, those of work, family, and leisure? The answer is that it can. For to the extent that well-being is fostered by enjoyment of and satisfaction with the activities of everyday life, the evidence suggests that well-being is an important by-product of serious leisure (Haworth, 1986; Haworth & Hill, 1992; Mannell, 1993). Furthermore, when interviewed, the respondents in my studies of serious leisure and those in many of the studies of other researchers reviewed in this book invariably described in detail and with great enthusiasm the satisfaction they get from their amateur, hobbyist, and volunteer involvements.

But all this evidence is correlational, for no one has carried out a study expressly designed to ascertain whether long-term involvement in a form of serious leisure leads to significant enduring increases in feelings of well-being. The extent to which serious leisure can generate intense interpersonal role conflict for some enthusiasts - it led to two divorces among the twenty-five respondents in the theatre study (Stebbins, 1979, pp. 81-83) - should be sufficient warning to avoid postulating an automatic link between this kind of leisure and well-being. I also have anecdotal evidence suggesting that serious leisure activities can generate intrapersonal conflict, such as when people fail to establish priorities among their many and varied leisure interests. Even an approach-approach conflict between two cherished leisure activities can possibly affect well-being unfavorably. Hamilton-Smith (1995, pp. 6-7) says our lack of knowledge about the link between serious leisure and well-being is a major lacuna in contemporary leisure research.

Finally, are we being realistic when we argue that serious leisure is a primary source of personal well-being in life? There is probably no sphere in life where well-being can take root and grow in pure, undiluted form. In other words, I suspect that when we are filled with feelings of well-being, whether at work, during leisure, or while performing nonwork obligations, we are, in effect, experiencing those feelings as a significant profit of rewards against costs. Moreover, what is noteworthy about the theoretical link between any kind of leisure and well-being is that, in common sense, we seldom expect costs in the former, whereas we routinely expect them at work and during the execution of obligatory tasks. That we expect to find pure enjoyment everywhere in our leisure, however unrealistic, may be shown someday to have a powerful effect on how much we enjoy, or are satisfied with or happy about, the serious leisure we pursue. And when a sense of well-being does emerge here - as it surely will - will this expectation influence the level of intensity with which the well-being is felt. Certainly, we can be mildly *or* highly satisfied with a serious pursuit or activity, enjoy it somewhat *or* enjoy it immensely.

Serious leisure and well-being would seem to make a perfect couple, but their relationship seems destined to be far more complicated than current levels of theory and research would

suggest.

Unemployment

Unemployment is by no means only about leisure. This is because unemployment does not automatically result in leisure for its victims; for them it automatically results only in free time, or time away from work and other obligations. Viewed from a different angle, unemployment is *forced* nonobligated time. As such it has raised in social science circles the question of whether a person in such circumstances can find stimulating, or true, leisure of any kind, be it casual or serious.

What evidence exists on the matter suggests that the experience of unemployment varies from person to person and according to the sorts of activities each turns to when trying to counteract its worst effects (Haworth, 1986, p. 288). Still, in comparison with the unemployed in the lower-level occupations, the unemployed in the upper-level occupations, including professionals, are more likely to look to serious leisure and in this manner ride out the dispiriting effects of their unfortunate economic situation. The former are more often overwhelmed by the act of being thrown out of work, suffering from depression and lethargy to the extent that pursuing leisure of any kind becomes next to impossible (Kay, 1990, p. 415). Part of the problem, it seems, is that they feel useless and pressured by social convention to search unceasingly for work, a frame of mind that virtually alienates them from true leisure. That is, they are too demoralized to engage in leisure, a purposive activity designed to achieve a particular end. Meanwhile, sitting around idle is no more leisure than it is work.

Boas Shamir (1985), in an Israeli study of unemployed men and women with university degrees, found that those with a strong Protestant ethic and work involvement were much more likely to turn to, and benefit from, leisure activities than those with a weaker ethic. Tess Kay (1990) studied a small, racially mixed subsample of men and women in Britain who, while unemployed, had developed a sustained interest in certain serious leisure activities. She concluded that, for them, the experience of unemployment had its positive side whereas, for the majority of unemployed people in her main sample, the experience was largely negative. Lobo and Watkins (1994) obtained similar results in Australia as did Haworth and Ducker (1991) in Britain.

Based on their research on caregivers, Weinblatt and Navon (1995), hypothesized that in certain situations people actually try to avoid leisure, feeling they have no right to it because, for example, it is self-interested, prevents meeting serious obligations, and compared with them, is trivial. The unemployed give similar reasons for abstaining from leisure. Thus the "flight from leisure" by them and by Weinblatt and Navon's caregivers raises at least two questions. One, should we try to promote leisure as a main avenue to well-being when it is unwanted? Two, can serious leisure engender well-being under these conditions, after caregivers and the unemployed, for example, are made aware of it and become willing to try it? My answer to the first question has always been "no" (e.g., Stebbins, 1998a, p. 18). As for the second question, I think we will only know the answer through careful research. True, serious leisure is anything but trivial, but it is also self-interested, and given its magnetic, appeal could prevent meeting obligations.

Retirement

Sooner or later most workers retire. Nevertheless, retirement itself may be partial or complete, and depending on the individual and his or her occupation, may occur at widely different stages of life. Thus, professional football players and ballet dancers typically retire around age thirty (Stebbins, 1993c, p. 131; Federico, 1983, p. 62), whereas professional painters and actors often work as long as their health and stamina hold up (Hearn, 1972). Among the latter, some pursue their professions into their eighties. Most organizationally-based workers, even though they may be performing well at the time, are forced to retire at a fixed age as established by law or by a private pension plan. Others, for whom work amounts to a necessary evil, lose enthusiasm for their jobs and opt for early retirement.

Whatever the age of retirement, adequate health and income condition the activities engaged in from thereon. To convey the broadest sense of what retirement means with reference to serious leisure, we consider in this section only those who retire with health, income, companionship, and transportation sufficient to participate in a wide range of leisure activities. These four requirements, and others, can, if not met, severely restrict the pursuit of leisure in old age (McDonald & Wanner, 1990, p. 92). As for the literature on the subject, it centers almost exclusively on partly- and fully-retired elderly workers. We know little about the retirement leisure of football players, ballet dancers, some military veterans, and the like who leave their jobs at a relatively young age and who, because they are not too old to enter a second, full-time occupational career in another field, can only pursue their leisure during the hours after work.

First it should be noted that, in certain occupational groups, significant numbers of workers never do retire, or they retire only partially. Managers, professionals, and self-employed people, are the most likely of all occupational categories to seek full- or part-time work at that time of life when most in their age bracket are interested in full retirement. In a national longitudinal study of American men in which they compared data gathered in 1966 and 1981, Parnes and his colleagues (1985, p. 92) found that 25.7 percent of the formally retired managers and professionals in their sample were working or looking for work, the highest percentage in any occupational category.[1] Moreover, "labor force participation tends to be higher immediately following retirement than it is after a number of years have elapsed. . . . Analysis of data by date of retirement . . . reveals no evidence of an upward trend in labor force participation over time either for the total group of retirees or for the health and voluntary retirees considered separately" (Parnes et al., 1985, p. 93) The attractive work and its generous remuneration helped explain the high rate of postretirement employment among the managers and professionals. The self-employed, professional or not, showed an equally high rate of postretirement employment; perhaps because they could arrange for flexible, part-time work schedules and avoid the confining regulations of private pension plans (in Canada, see Schellenberg, 1994, p. 37). And, according to the Parnes et al study, men whose wives are still working outside the home are also more inclined to look for work in their early postretirement years.

The respondents in the aforementioned study, whatever their former occupations, gave two main reasons for seeking employment during formal retirement: the need for money and the need for something to do (Parnes et al., 1985, pp. 97-98). Yet, although the vast majority of men in their postretirement years had no interest in working more, the proportion of men who did express either a categorical or a conditional interest in a postretirement job was significantly higher among those who had worked in managerial or professional positions than among those who had worked in other occupations. Nonetheless, the unfavorable stereotypes of elderly workers, such as their presumed inaccuracy, inconsistency, and absenteeism, discourage even some professionals from seeking paid employment beyond formal retirement (Sheppard, 1976).

Within these patterns of full and partial retirement, elderly retirees tend to continue with the leisure they have come to enjoy in their earlier years (Kelly, 1997, pp. 168-169), even though aging eventually limits participation in some activities. Roadburg (1985, p. 85), in a study conducted in Canada, found that older people were most likely to maintain or increase their rate of participation only in activities requiring little expense and physical exertion. This means that, as they age and their health and energy decline, they are increasingly likely to conduct their activities indoors and at home, and for the very old, alone (McPherson, 1990, p. 434). Few people who retire in their sixties or later take up an unfamiliar form of leisure.

Mannell's study (1993) of Canadian retirees revealed that the pursuit of "high investment" activities pays off in the currency of significant life satisfaction. High investment leisure activities require commitment, obligation, some discipline, and even occasional sacrifice; they are, in effect, serious leisure. Mannell's analyses provide support for the hypothesis that those older adults who are more satisfied with their lives invest greater effort (indicated by experiencing flow) in more of their daily activities than those who report less satisfaction with their lives. This high investment . . . however, was not guaranteed simply by participating in more potentially high-investment activities such as volunteer work, sport and exercise, home maintenance, hobbies, travel, and cultural pursuits. When participation was voluntary, the occurrence of flow in these activities was mediated by the presence or absence of a sense of commitment or obligation to participate (Mannell, 1993, p. 141).

He concluded that some people may need to feel a certain external push (commitment, obligation) to overcome their psychological resistance to pursuing activities that require an investment of effort.

Of the three types of serious leisure, career volunteering is possibly the one most widely pursued and most highly valued by the elderly, who were found in a survey conducted by the American Association of Retired Persons (1988) to engage in it 20 percent more than any other age category. A similar study revealed that only 24 percent of the sample refused the opportunity to perform volunteer work of some kind (Independent Sector, 1988, p. 35). Among the elderly, retired professionals and other upper-middle class workers in good health volunteer more than others their age (Lambing, 1972; Walker, Kimmel, & Price, 1980-1981).

On a related note, Fischer and Schaffer (1993, pp. 18-21) concluded from their review of the literature that whether an older person volunteers depends on his or her social class; in other words the propensity to volunteer increases with income, education, and occupational status. Chambré (1987, p. 89) found education to be the most important of these variables. Nevertheless, in keeping with the tendency for leisure choices to be continuous across the adult lifespan, those who join voluntary associations or who work as volunteers during old age were usually joiners and volunteers during midlife (McPherson, 1990, pp. 438-39). This kind of leisure tends to peak somewhere between 10 years before and 10 years after retirement, beyond which it declines in harmony with the tendency for leisure to become increasingly solitary and home-based.

The Independent Sector study (1988, p. 35), which examined the motives of elderly volunteers representing all occupational backgrounds, revealed that they volunteer for four main reasons: a) they want something interesting to do (56 percent), b) think they will enjoy the work (40 percent), c) have religious concerns (27 percent), or d) have plenty of free time (14 percent). Their reasons for continuing to volunteer were much the same, except that the free time motive was replaced with another motive: having an interest in the activity (28 percent). With the possible exception of the motive of religious concerns, the reasons for volunteering at this age level clearly square with the argument presented elsewhere in this volume that volunteering is seen much of the time by the volunteers themselves as a form of leisure.

Gender roles also influence the kinds of volunteering men and women do in retirement (Fischer, Mueller, & Cooper, 1991): Women are more likely to be affiliated with or volunteer for church, school, cultural, and hobbyist groups, whereas men are attracted to sport, service, fraternal, veterans, and job-related associations. As for the question of who among the elderly volunteers more, men or women, the findings are contradictory (Fischer & Schaffer, 1993, p. 21).

The liberal arts hobbies have special import for retired professionals, even though we have yet to discover the rates at which they and other retired workers participate in them. Nevertheless, to the extent that they seek less enervating activities at home or indoors, common sense suggests that retirees from many of the professions would be especially interested in this kind of activity. For instance, recent research demonstrates that middle- and upper-class elderly people participate more in adult learning programs than those from the lower-class. We saw earlier that when considered together these programs cover an immense array of hobbies and amateur activities. In 1983 Deveraux (1985, p. 55) estimated that four percent of Canadians sixty-five years of age and older were enrolled in one or more credit or noncredit courses in continuing education. The credit courses were offered at both the graduate and the undergraduate levels, but only a small proportion of these students were seeking credit for them. The University of the Third Age, founded in

France in 1974, now offers on a world-wide basis instruction of this kind for the elderly. Meanwhile the Elderhostel Program, which consists of one- to two-week noncredit courses, is presently available in over forty countries. It stands as still another form of self-directed education of the liberal arts hobby variety, apparently attracting retired professionals in exceptional numbers.

On the policy level, Kelly (1997, p. 177) proposes that retirees be encouraged to try to "direct their lives in a balance of engagement that is at least relatively satisfying." To be sure, this assumes adequate health, income, companionship, and transportation. It also assumes that the elderly know there are leisure activities that can be seriously pursued, a tall order perhaps, since a Canadian study suggests that they see leisure chiefly in casual terms (Roadburg, 1985, p. 69). But when these conditions are met, older people, as Mannell (1993) has now demonstrated, are capable of pursuing many kinds of serious leisure (e.g., Osgood, 1997; Williamson, 1995; Stebbins, 1978) and through it attaining a higher level of satisfaction in life than otherwise. Kelly (1993, p. 177) observes that "the process of constriction that characterizes later life may at least be delayed by opportunities that are both possible and satisfying."

Serious Leisure outside the First World[2]

The issue of serious leisure outside the First World stands apart from the preceding four issues in that, to my knowledge, it has never been raised in the literature, that is, it has not yet emerged as a matter of debate among researchers. But it has stirred comment among students, notably those in the international masters program of the World Leisure and Recreation Centre of Excellence (WICE), where I have taught from time to time since its inception in 1992. Their views of the role, frequency, and dispersion of serious leisure in their countries have been illuminating.

The greatest contrasts exist between the First and Third Worlds. Students from Asia, Africa, and Latin America, for example, believe that serious leisure is much rarer in their countries, and some forms of it hardly seem to exist at all. They acknowledge the existence of amateur sport, but not amateur science. Amateur art and entertainment are vague ideas for them, since both fields merge with their folkloristic counterparts. Collecting as serious leisure is largely a foreign idea to them, as are the liberal arts hobbies and nearly all the activities classified as activity participation (hunting, fishing, and the folk arts being exceptions). More familiar is the hobby of making things, particularly making baskets, clothing, and pottery and raising animals. But with the making and participation activities that they do know, there is, in a way similar to the arts and entertainment fields, a blurring of the line separating what is obligatory from what is leisure. The concept of competitive sports, games, and contests is familiar, but the activities themselves, which are so common in the First World, are much less so. Some students speak of amateur and hobbyist serious leisure as being available only to their country's elite, whose leisure tastes have been influenced by the West.

Students from the Third world recognize the practice of volunteering, but hold that it is enacted differently there. Organizational volunteering is much less common than the grass roots type, while informal volunteering - helping - appears to be considerably more common than either of these two formal kinds. Even here the line separating obligation and voluntary action is fuzzy in ways largely unknown in the First World. For example, in some countries, the expectation of helping is institutionalized, as seen in the practice found in parts of Columbia where every man in the village is obligated to help when one of them builds a house.

Students from the Second World countries (those of the former Communist bloc), seem to look on serious leisure in much the same way as those from the First World. Nevertheless, the milieu within which it is pursued is dramatically different, given the vast social, economic, and cultural adjustments that have been taking place since the communist system started formally unravelling in the latter half of the 1980s. In other words, in this part of the globe, participation in serious leisure is as much in flux as participation in the rest of life. Given the scope, subtlety, and evanescence of these adjustments, students from these countries have found it difficult to identify their effects on serious leisure there. Jung offers a good description of the present situation in Poland, thereby suggesting what it may be like in other Second World countries:

> These new issues include the problem of commercialization of leisure provision and its privatization, a growing stratification of leisure consumers by income rather than education due to a rapid polarization of wealth, and lack of economic and personal security in the face of unemployment, soaring crime rates and the appearance of new forms of organized crime, hitherto unknown in Poland (Jung, 1996, p. 192)

He also comments on the tendency to participate less in the collective and socialized forms of leisure and more in those based at home or in privatized facilities. Furthermore, this trend is nurturing the growth of individualized leisure, which hints at a possible upswing in the pursuit of the predominantly self-interested forms of serious leisure, the hobbies and amateur activities.

The lesson in all this is clear: research and theorizing in serious leisure, which has so far has come almost exclusively from the First World, is by no means always generalizable to countries outside it. The WICE students have identified some of the areas where we must exercise caution.

Conclusions

A common thread knits together the five issues covered in this chapter, notably, the observation that leisure is in no way a unitary phenomenon. I have argued here that careers exist in serious but not in casual leisure, that serious leisure may be capable of engendering a special kind of well-being, that such leisure can offer special opportunities for the unemployed and the retired in ways other leisure cannot. I have also argued that, outside the First World, serious leisure has a special place when compared with casual leisure.

Yet the conventional approach to leisure studies, which is to treat leisure as though it were a unitary phenomenon, has been precisely the opposite of the one taken in this chapter. In other words, in this generic approach, theories and propositions are intended to explain all leisure, and research is conducted to examine leisure from a single overarching definition or from a list of activities believed to be representative of leisure as a whole. This approach fails to tell the entire story, however, for it fails to distinguish the components of meaning associated with the immediate experience of particular leisure activities in particular situations (Kelly & Godbey, 1992, p. 234). For instance, some unemployed people *do* find leisure attractive, but the appeal lies in serious rather than casual leisure. One of the reasons for developing the distinction between casual and serious leisure, which is most thoroughly described in chapter 4, was to show that all leisure is not cut from the same cloth; that many important differences are being masked by the prevailing generic analyses and theories which treat leisure as a unitary phenomenon.

Leisure varies widely according to type of activity, be it casual or serious. Moreover, when leisure is studied by type, rather than generically, many important qualities of the different types become evident. The dual classification of serious leisure and casual leisure and its several subtypes, a distinction expressly created to highlight some of the fundamental differences between leisure activities, is ideally suited for developing a body of knowledge that complements what we have learned about leisure from studying it generically.

My antigeneric approach, which we could label the "typological approach," does admittedly lead to a proliferation of types and subtypes, causing displeasure among at least some of those who want to talk only in general terms. But such proliferation is unavoidable; developing a classification of basic phenomena is the first step in every science, where however, the classification must be founded on valid distinguishing criteria and consist of types that are theoretically important. The three main types serious leisure meet these two criteria, as do the several subtypes of amateurs and hobbyists, for all these types emerged inductively through direct research as part of grounded theory. Although many examples of the importance of the types can be found throughout this book, let me recall just two more. First, with respect to people who are elderly or have a disability, it often makes more sense to try to interest them in the liberal arts hobbies than in many of the other kinds of serious leisure or in leisure in general. Second, leisure education, at bottom, is not about all leisure but only about serious leisure.

Of course there are times when we do want to speak of leisure as a unitary phenomenon. The studies of proportions of work and leisure time are possibly the best example of this. Geographic and economic analyses of leisure, in many instances anyway, can be conducted without invoking the typological approach. But there are also many branches of leisure studies where, were this approach to be used, it would greatly enrich our understanding of, for example, meaning, constraints, motivation, and adaptation to unemployment. Moreover, typological distinctions are absolutely essential in examining the role of leisure in the job-reduced future.

Part IV The Twenty-First Century

Chapter 10

The Job-Reduced Future

In the industrialized world of today, there is more time after work than ever. Still, it was true for awhile in the United States, as Schor (1991) concluded in *The Overworked American*, that many of them were so eager to make money to buy coveted items that they took second jobs or worked overtime whenever possible, striving in the meantime to save money through do-it-yourself projects. After meeting the multitude of obligations they had set for themselves, these drudges found themselves with scarcely any free time. Only four years later, however, Howe (1995) claimed that this attitude is changing; now more and more American workers are emphasizing "reasoned wellness" while backing off from their earlier greed and narcissism. She held that they are also beginning to endow family time with the same level of importance as work and other forms of obligated time. In a similar vein, Samuel (1994a, p. 48) described the tendency observed by Schor as a "temporary development" in the United States that stands out against the world-wide trend toward increased free time.

Overall, American research does support the claim that the after-work time of many people has been growing both in amount and significance (Robinson and Godbey, 1997). But, oddly, this research also suggests that some of them feel more rushed than ever. Zuzanek (1996, p. 65) provides the clearest statement yet of this paradox. "In general, US time-budget findings parallel those of Canada, and provide additional evidence of the complexity of life in modern industrial societies marked, as it seems, by concurrent trends toward greater time freedom as well as 'harriedness' and 'time pressure.'" And this general trend persists despite the present tendency in a number of industries for managers to wring many extra hours of service from their full-time salaried and hourly-rated employees.[1] Yet, the size of this group of reluctantly overworked employees is shrinking as more and more of their positions are lost in the nearly universal shuffle to organize as much work as possible along electronic lines.

Lefkowitz (1979) prefigured this trend - the willful and substantial reduction of life's work and nonwork obligations. His interviews, conducted during the late 1970s, suggested that a small but growing number of Americans were expanding their leisure involvements by voluntarily accepting unemployment, partial employment, or early retirement. Two years later Yankelovich (1981) confirmed these impressions in a nationwide survey of Americans. Today, the evidence clearly supports the proposition that the work ethic of old is waning in intensity, even in North America, the home of the largest number of its adherents by far.

Now, parallelling the tendency to voluntarily reduce obligations is a much stronger force: the technologically-driven, involuntary reduction of paid work. In *The End of Work* Jeremy Rifkin (1995) describes the current decline in the size of the global labor pool and the traditional market economy and how both forces are now pushing ever larger numbers of people toward greater free time at an alarming rate, whatever the individual's interest in reducing his or her level of work. As the twenty-first century dawns, a wide variety of employable men and women are finding that their job opportunities have shrunk, sometimes to nothing at all. Behind these unsettling trends lie the powerful forces of what Rifkin calls the "Third Industrial Revolution": the far-reaching effects of electronic technology as manifested in the microcircuitry of computers, robotics, telecommunications, and similar devices.

The Information Age has dawned. In it, Rifkin observes, these technologies will continue well into the twenty-first century inexorably replacing workers, either directly or indirectly, in virtually every sector of the economy, including manufacturing, transportation, agriculture, government, and the retail and financial services. New jobs will be created in significant number only in the knowledge sector, in science, computing, consulting, education, and the technical and professional services directly related to the new technology. Rifkin says this sector will compose no more than twenty percent of the workforce. Jobs lost in the other sectors will be gone forever, offset very little by the comparatively small number of jobs generated in the knowledge sector. And occupational retraining is no solution, for the people in line for such retraining generally lack the necessary educational background on which to build the skills and information they would need to work in the knowledge sector. In short, regardless of the orientation of the modern man and woman toward life after work, he and she now seems destined to have much more of it than ever. Two other books published by Aronowitz and DiFazio (1994) and Howard (1995) indicate that Rifkin is not alone in observing these trends.[2]

These writers have failed to address themselves to this question, apart from putting forward two broad observations, one tantalizing, the other frightening. They predict that the Information Age will offer greatly expanded opportunities for leisure and personal development by way of it and that this Age will offer free time far in excess of the typical person's capacity to use it constructively.[3] Seen from the standpoint of the person trying to adapt to a world buffeted by momentous change, these observers paint a picture of life after work in the Information Age that is both too hazy and too unsettling for comfort.

The task I have set for myself in this chapter is to complete this picture, sharpen its focus, and move beyond these two observations to set out the kinds of interesting and satisfying activities open to people in their time after work. To this end, I describe how serious leisure can serve as a nonremunerated substitute for work, showing in the process that people can transmute this time into an optimal leisure lifestyle.

Serious Leisure as a Substitute for Work

To start, we must return to the concept of social world introduced in chapter 1, the set of characteristic groups, events, routines, practices, and organizations, which is held together, to an important degree, by semiformal, or mediated, communication. The social world is not only a concept well in tune with the work and leisure routines of the present and future, it is also a desideratum of many a modern man and woman both for today and for the years to come. If people can no longer find a work organization to belong to or can only belong marginally to one as an outside consultant or part-time employee how, then, can they become part of the community, whether conceived of locally, regionally, nationally, or internationally? Increasingly, it appears that the only available communal connections for most people will come through activities taking place in their after-work time. Yet, because they tend to be private, purely family activities rarely generate such connections. But those who once found meaningful organizational ties at work can still turn to serious leisure, where one of the principal attractions of most of the amateur, hobbyist, and volunteer activities is the sense of being part of a bustling, fascinating, all-encompassing social world. For many enthusiasts this involvement is as exciting as the central activity itself and, in career volunteer work, often indistinguishable from it.

The routine of some serious leisure can constitute yet another appealing feature for those with severely shortened workweeks or no work at all. A wide variety of amateur activities require regular practice and rehearsal sessions, and volunteers are often asked to serve at their posts during certain hours on certain days of the week. People who miss the routine of the full-time job can find a satisfying equivalent in a variety of serious leisure pursuits.

Substitute Lifestyle and Identity

We also saw earlier that serious leisure offers a major lifestyle and identity for its participants, and I should now like to add that both can serve as solid substitutes for the ones they once knew in their work. Moreover, some lifestyles serve to identify their participants. In other words, the participants are members of a category of humankind who recognize themselves and, to some extent, are recognized by the larger community for the distinctive mode of life they lead. This is certainly true for the enthusiasts in some of the casual and many of the serious leisure activities.

It was observed in chapter 1 that a profound lifestyle awaits anyone routinely pursuing a serious leisure career in, say, amateur theatre, volunteer work with the mentally handicapped, the hobby of model railroading, or that of mountain climbing. And this person may also find exciting, albeit clearly less profound, lifestyles in such casual leisure pastimes as socializing in the local pub and drinking with golfing associates at the "nineteenth hole." But many other forms of casual leisure, for example, beachcombing or window shopping, are seldom shared with large numbers of other people; therefore they fail to qualify as group lifestyles as set out earlier. Moreover, in themselves, these activities are too superficial and unremarkable to serve as the basis for a recognizable mode of living where lifestyle is part of identity.

Substitute Central Life Interest

Finally, we have seen that, to the extent that lifestyles form around complicated, absorbing, satisfying activities, they can also be viewed as behavioral expressions of the participants' central life interests (Dubin, 1992) in those activities. In the Information Age with its dwindling employment opportunities, most men and women will find more and more that the only kinds of central life interests open to them are the various amateur, hobbyist, and career volunteer activities composing serious leisure. Additionally, more and more of the underemployed will find themselves with a choice never before encountered in the history of work in the industrialized world: whether to make their, say, twenty-five-hour-a-week job their central life interest or turn to a serious leisure activity for this kind of attachment because the job is too insubstantial for an investment of positive emotional, physical, and intellectual energy. Of course, for the unemployed and the retired, serious leisure is their only recourse if they are to have a central life interest at all. And there will always be a small number of people with sufficient time, energy, and opportunity to sustain more than one central life interest in either leisure or work and leisure.

As happens with leisure lifestyle, a leisure identity arises in conjunction with a leisure-based central life interest. In other words, the lifestyle of the participants in a given serious leisure activity expresses their central life interest there and forms the basis for their personal and communal identity as people who go in for that activity. In the future, jobless or relatively jobless as it will be for many people, serious leisure will be the only remaining area in life where they can find an identity related to their distinctive personal qualities, qualities expressed in the course of realizing the rewards and benefits of serious leisure. Moreover, in the Information Age, it will be the only remaining area where these people can find a community role capable of fostering significant self-respect. When seen in the light of the importance of work in Western society, most of the casual leisure activities with their strong appeal of immediate intrinsic reward are usually dismissed as adding little to their participants' self-respect.

The Contributions of Serious Leisure

Just as they do at work, serious leisure participants also make a number of important contributions to self and to the community. One of these comes through the social worlds associated with the different forms of this leisure, wherein each type of member (stranger, tourist, regular, insider) finds a distinctive sense of belonging and participation. This sense stands out in relief in the author's studies in this field. It is also evident in Mittelstaedt's (1995) detailed description of the types of participants inhabiting the bustling social world of American Civil War reenactments. Here each type gains immense satisfaction from his or her own special involvements.

Additionally, to the extent it is pursued with other people, serious leisure can contribute significantly to communal and even societal integration. For example, Thompson (1992) found that the members of a women's tennis association in Australia, who met weekly for matches, came from a range of different social classes and age groups. In a similar vein, as part of the observational component of a study of francophone volunteers, I sat on the board of directors of a French-language community organization composed of a realtor, teacher, banker, homemaker, data analyst, business executive, high school student, and myself, a sociologist and university professor. There was also a nearly equal representation of the two sexes who, together, ranged in age from sixteen to around sixty-five. Likewise, Parker (1994) describes how certain kinds of volunteers, when they exercise their citizenship rights by taking an active part in running the society in which they live, contribute to communal integration at the same time.

Many serious leisure groups also have a far reaching salutary effect on the general welfare of the community. Put more concisely, they benefit their publics in such important ways as performing with a community orchestra or hosting a "star night" through the local astronomical society. The latter event is open to anyone interested in observing the evening sky with the portable telescopes of the society's amateur members. Finnegan (1989) describes for a single community (the English new town of Milton Keynes) the complex, positive effect on the different music publics of entire local amateur-professional-hobbyist music scene.

The Importance of Organizations

The work, or more accurately, the nonwork situation of many people in the Information Age will consist, in part, of being cast adrift from the key organizational moorings of their employment days, a clear sign of a "post-traditional existence" (Stebbins, 1996e). More and more these people will find themselves floating, with no rudder, in an organizationless sea, a result of their unemployment, retirement, or marginal affiliation with a work organization as a temporary consultant or limited-term contractual worker. It is true that this absence of organizational ties will likely pose little or no problem for some people; their family relationships and friendship networks are all they will ever want. Others, however, may well miss the sense of belonging to a collectivity with greater public visibility and integration than networks and relationships typically have. If this proposition turns out to be true, being cut off from the organizational belongingness they once enjoyed at work will inspire these former employees to search for other organizations capable of replacing this loss.

Although there are forms of serious leisure with little or no organizational structure, most notably the liberal arts hobbies, the vast majority of these forms present much the opposite tendency. People seeking new organizational ties can find elaborate social worlds in the latter, consisting of clubs, associations, commercial dealers, useful services, organized routine events, and on and on.[*] Volunteers nearly always work in or for an organization of some kind. The main exceptions here are the votaries who serve as volunteers in a social movement so new that a formal organizational structure has not yet evolved. In addition, the various leisure organizations provide socially visible rallying points for the individualized leisure identities of their members as well as outlets for the central life interests they share. Furthermore, a club, team, orchestra, or society commonly serves as the hub or one important hub of the lifestyle enjoyed by the participants pursuing the associated serious leisure activity.

The casual leisure activities are unable fill this craving for organizational belonging, for they rarely if ever become formally organized. Participants here retain too much of their former character as consumer masses to serve as the seedbed for formal groups and organizations. There is, of course, a true sense of belonging that comes with sharing private symbols with other members of the same mass (Maffesoli, 1996, pp. 76-77, 96-100), but the sense of solidarity that comes with belonging to an organization is commonly missing in casual leisure.

These concluding remarks indicate that today's serious leisure can offer a multitude of benefits in the job-reduced future now faced or soon to be faced by many inhabitants of the industrialized world.

Chapter 11

New Directions in Research

In chapter 9 we tackled several theoretical and practical issues about which, over the years, there has been a certain amount of discussion. The new directions in research considered in the present chapter differ, however, in that they have not been the object of scholarly debate (at least within leisure studies), but rather that they have been suggested by one or more people as new and fruitful lines of investigation that should be pursued soon. Seven new directions in research in serious leisure are covered here: flow, play, and serious leisure; culture of commitment; adolescents and serious leisure; gendered experiences in serious leisure; leisure education; community development and participative citizenship; and serious leisure societies. This list is not meant to be exhaustive. It is likely there are other new directions that have escaped my attention.

Flow, Play, and Serious Leisure

Hamilton-Smith (1992) helped set the stage for one important research agenda when he observed that serious leisure activities, because many of them encourage play, exploration, and aesthetic appreciation, are especially likely to generate optimal psychological arousal, or flow (see chapter 1). Unaware of Hamilton-Smith's proposition, I published a similar one the same year (see Stebbins, 1992, pp. 112, 127), and then, several years later, elaborated on it for jazz, barbershop, and classical music:

> The benefits of enrichment, expression, and renewal of self are especially

strong in these arts because of the vivid "flow experience" they can provide for those who perform them. When in flow while performing, the person's awareness merges with the action of creating the music to form a single sensation. Attention comes to be centered exclusively on the all-absorbing process of producing the music. A person in flow tends to lose his or her sense of self and to become wrapped up in the musical action of the immediate present (Stebbins, 1996a, p. 8).

Moreover, in retrospect, I could have described in the same terms certain moments in the lives of amateur and professional archaeologists, astronomers, stand-up comics, entertainment magicians, and football and baseball players.

But these have been, or would have been, *ex-post-facto* interpretations of respondents' comments made during interviews or on the spot while I was observing them in their serious leisure. No data have yet been reported from direct examination of the hypothesis that, at particular points in time, all or a significant proportion of serious leisure generates flow for its participants. This having been said, just such a study is underway at the University of Alberta, where doctoral student Robert Kassian has been interviewing amateur dancers about the flow they experience in performing their art. His research should reveal a multitude of new details about the complex relationship between this psychological process and serious leisure.

Culture of Commitment

In 1993, Alan Tomlinson (1993) issued a call for research on the "culture of commitment," which is evident in many a serious leisure activity. The term refers to the commitment people have to particular collective forms of everyday life, among them sports teams, arts groups, and volunteer projects. It differs from the commitment of personally-felt obligation, such as that observed by Mannell (1993) in his study of serious leisure participation among the elderly. It also differs from personal value commitment, or value attachment, as discussed in chapter 1 (see also Stebbins, 1992, pp. 51-52) and examined elsewhere in this book by Yair, Shamir, and others. Rather Tomlinson's collective form of commitment revolves around the attachment of individuals to groups and to what they can do for those groups, as opposed to what they can gain from the groups for themselves. True, the second two forms of commitment can sometimes be expressed in the same action, as when a community orchestra violinist practices diligently to experience the satisfaction of playing well at the next concert, while helping the group reach one of its principal goals: the production of high quality music. By contrast, purely collective commitment is evident when the same musician, though he or she is well enough prepared to need no additional work, nevertheless reports for a special rehearsal called for the purpose of improving the performance of the violin section.

I am not aware of anyone heeding Tomlinson's call, perhaps because his ideas have received insufficient publicity. Its lack of recognition notwithstanding, a solid comprehension of the attitude of collective commitment and the culture in which it is embedded and expressed would be invaluable. Although the modern age is dominated by individualism, it also an age where group efforts are as important as ever. Therefore, we cannot afford to ignore these two ideas, since they help form the basis for altruism, participative citizenship, and community development and integration. They also add to our knowledge of the mesostructural and sociocultural levels of serious leisure participation described in chapter 1. Both levels are deficient in research when compared with the personal and interactional levels.

Adolescents and Serious Leisure

With but two exceptions, there has been no research on the serious leisure of adolescents, the two exceptions being Corrine Spector's masters thesis project presently being completed at Bar-Ilan University in Israel and my own exploration of Canadian magicians, the amateur component of which included a handful of seventeen-year-old males. In this regard, I should like to point out that the samples of these two studies are inconsistent with my earlier pronouncement about the logical place of nonadults in serious leisure:

> It follows that amateurs are normally adults, although in some fields they may be older teenagers as well (as happened in the study of magicians). In general, however, only other adults can be functionally related to professionals in the ways set forth earlier. Thus, children's activities are best described not by the term "amateur," but by other descriptors, such as "youth" orchestra, "peewee" hockey, "childrens" art, and so forth (Stebbins, 1992, p.

41)

It is possible that this statement has discouraged some researchers from examining the amateur activities of adolescents, if not the entire spectrum of serious leisure of interest to them.

A part from this matter of inconsistency, my earlier statement now seems needlessly restrictive as well. Even if they are seldom, or never, involved with professionals as adult amateurs can be and often are, some adolescents do nevertheless appear to pursue forms of serious leisure with adult-like passion, commitment, and perseverance, and like older participants, they may be marginalized for doing so by the dominant casual leisure climate. Thus we should also be striving to learn about, for instance, the lifestyles and social worlds of teenagers active in all types of serious leisure and about how they manage their leisure as full-time students and participants in family and peer-group activities.

Furthermore, for society, the payoff of knowledge about adolescent involvement in serious leisure could be considerable. For example, what role does such involvement play in promoting adolescent well-being, preventing antisocial behavior (see Stebbins 1998c), and establishing lifelong patterns of deep leisure satisfaction? It is possible that adolescents who pursue a form of serious leisure serve as leisure role models for their peers, unless, of course, they are qualified as "weird" because they participate noticeably less often in casual leisure than the rest. Systematic research in this area is long overdue, and I hope my earlier statement has not contributed to this deficiency.

Gendered Experiences in Serious Leisure

Raisborough (1999) has observed that research on serious leisure has tended to neglect the question of gendered experiences there, even creating the impression in some quarters that this form of leisure is a male only undertaking. Even though the involvements of women were explicitly described and analyzed in the fieldwork on stand-up comics (Stebbins, 1990) and barbershop singers (Stebbins, 1996: chap. 6) and more sporadically explored in some of my other studies, her observation is nevertheless generally valid: there has been significant neglect of the question of gendered experiences in serious leisure. Her investigation of amateurs in Britain's Sea Cadet Corps (SCC) shows how this neglect can obscure important data.

One of her most intriguing findings is that, in the SCC, women more often than men fail to recognize its activities as a form of leisure. Instead, the regular routines of the SCC facilitate what these women define as their own leisure, various forms of casual leisure involving neither the SCC nor their family or home. It was the regular routines of this organization that enabled these women to set aside time for a kind of leisure seen as rightfully theirs. Without anyway denying the importance of Raisborough's plea for more research on the gendered experience of serious leisure, it is possible, as I found in studying key volunteers, that some of the cadets conceive of leisure only in casual terms but would redefine their SCC activities as serious leisure if they were instructed about this idea (Stebbins, 1998d). Nevertheless, feminist analysis of serious leisure is an important new direction in this field.

Leisure Education

Everyone, whether adolescent or adult, is aware of at least a couple of forms of serious leisure, even if he or she is quite unlikely to refer to them by this term. But rare indeed among the general public are people whose understanding of serious leisure is deep enough to inspire them to organize their lives in such a way that they can experience optimal leisure satisfaction. The broad nescience of serious leisure prompted the founding in 1977 of the branch of the World Leisure and Recreation Association known as the Commission on Education. It is guided by three objectives: 1) to promote awareness of the significance of leisure and recreation, 2) to promote and foster quality research in leisure education, and 3) to disseminate information on leisure education. In addition, the Commission's Charter contains the statement that "leisure education is a lifelong learning process which incorporates the development of leisure attitudes, values, knowledge, skills and resources" (quoted from p. 5).

At this point it is in order to repeat what I said earlier: for the most part, leisure education should center on serious leisure. It should consist mainly of imparting knowledge about the nature of serious leisure, about its costs and rewards, and about participating in particular serious leisure activities. I also noted that this conception of leisure education intentionally excludes casual leisure, since such leisure requires little or no training or encouragement to partake of it and find enjoyment there.

Although the policy and practice of leisure education has been around for several decades, education in serious leisure as just described is in its infancy.[1] It constitutes therefore another new direction in which the perspective may go, where it would, however, center on policy and practice rather than on research. Meanwhile, literature in this area is scarce. To date, my book *After Work* (Stebbins, 1998a) is the only written statement available on education for serious leisure. It was written with two audiences in mind. One consists of those self-directed learners who are searching for an optimal leisure lifestyle. The other consists of leisure practitioners and students in leisure studies and adult education who would like to help the first to realize their free-time goals.

Community Development and Participative Citizenship

Using the scenario of the Information Age as his backdrop, in much the same way as we did in the preceding chapter, Reid (1995) argues that leisure can no longer be viewed solely as idle, casual, frivolous, and self-indulgent, but that it must now also be viewed as purposeful, in particular, as activity leading to individual as well as community development. These two together, he says, compose the foundation for participative citizenship, wherein citizens contribute in positive ways to the functioning of their community. Reid sees serious leisure as the kind of activity that will form the central part of this foundation:

> Much of work today is only useful in that it provides a means to a livelihood. New forms of individual and community contribution will become possible once the market is no longer the only mechanism for judging contribution. Many activities which are now done a voluntary basis could be enhanced so that the community and those in need benefit. To do so requires new forms of social organization which place greater worth on those services. This is the essence of Stebbins' notion of serious leisure (Reid, 1995, pp. 112-113).

Reid goes on to note that this need for new social organization is an especially important legacy of the Post-Materialist society in which we now live.

In fact, several of the contributions that amateurs, hobbyists, and career volunteers can make to the community have already been described (see chapters 3 and 10). Moreover, we have seen that contributing to the success of a collective project and to the maintenance and development of the group (in this instance the community) are two main rewards of serious leisure. Thus the central role of serious leisure in participative citizenship has been recognized, not only in principle by Reid, and somewhat earlier by Parker (1994), but also in concrete detail in this book as well as in a chapter by Mason-Mullet (1996). The latter discusses a number of career volunteer projects, which over the years, have led to community development, projects that she says can be understood as leisure activities.[2]

What remains to be done - and this is why I have placed the discussion of community development and participative citizenship in this chapter on new directions - is to systematically explore all the contributions that the various forms of serious leisure can make to collective life. In this regard, the previously-mentioned study of citizen participation in planning for healthy communities (career volunteering) conducted by Arai and Pedlar (1997) could serve as a useful model.

Serious Leisure Societies

Among First World nations, Dutch society presents the closest ratio of free time to obligated time where, in 1985, according to de Vroom and Blomsma (1991), the working and nonworking segments of the population were nearly equal in size. The working segment - estimated at 52.3 percent - includes unemployed members of the labor force who were looking for work when surveyed. The Dutch program of a guaranteed minimum income and paid holidays, which is available even to nonworking adults, helps to account for this ratio (Richards, 1996). These data suggest that the Dutch have more free time than people living in other First World countries.

I used these proportions as a springboard for developing a paper in which I hypothesized that the Netherlands, seen with reference to the other societies in the First World, is the society with the greatest per capita interest in serious leisure (Stebbins, 1998b). Now, there is no way that the miscellaneous data presented in that paper can stand on their own as evidence confirming this hypothesis. They are, in effect, quantitative exploratory data suggesting that the hypothesis is plausible (more than a mere figment of its author's imagination). But it *is* a hypothesis, and to establish its full validity, we must test it more rigorously and systematically using controlled research.

I should like to propose a research program consisting of an extensive cross-national comparison of rates of participation in a sample of serious leisure activities in First World countries.[3] The sample should be representative of the three main types of serious leisure as well as their principal subtypes, and would have to be restricted to those activities on which comparative cross-national quantitative data could be gathered and on which we already have ethnographic data. In amateurism, for example, we could gather data from, say, Western European and North American countries, on theatre and classical music (art), astronomy and archaeology (science), magic (entertainment) and, soccer (sport), although the last of these is comparatively weakly represented in Canada and the United States. Each of these activities is organized and each has accessible membership lists capable of offering for every country studied a general picture of the rate of involvement there. With the exception of soccer, the ethnographic context of these activities and their meaning for participants has already been explored although, given the North American basis of this research, a validity check is recommended in selected European countries.[4]

Conclusions

The directions of future research set out in this chapter, to the extent they are followed, are likely to bring not only new empirical data but also significant theoretical advances. It is certainly possible, for example, that the list of ten rewards or the three-fold classification of types of costs (tensions, dislikes, disappointments) could be further expanded through research along these lines. Such research should also enable us to deepen considerably our understanding of the contributions that serious leisure makes to the community. But most important of all, perhaps, is the possibility that the new avenues will lead to further elaboration of the structural and sociocultural levels of analysis, to this point the least developed of the five levels of the serious leisure perspective.

Moving off in new directions of research means retaining the exploratory-qualitative methodological approach used to establish the grounded theoretic basis of serious leisure through the studies of amateurs, hobbyists, and francophone key volunteers. Where we know little about the field being examined, it is wise to explore it in an open-ended manner to ensure that all relevant processes and structures are identified and considered.[5] Assuming this advice is accepted, the time will eventually come when controlled, confirmatory-quantitative research will be needed, for example, to add precision to certain inductively-generated propositions and to eliminate the contradictions found in rival hypotheses. There is also a need for survey research on the frequency of serious leisure activities in various populations as well as on the nature of their demographic correlates.

In the more established areas of the serious leisure perspective, researchers are now starting to test certain hypotheses (e.g., Juniu et al., 1996; Goff et al., 1997), a welcome procedure since there is a foundation of grounded theory to work from. Although many facets of serious leisure have yet to be explored and many serious leisure activities exist about which we know little, it is heartening to see the perspective mature in some of its aspects to the point where open-ended methodology is no longer required. Nevertheless, it seems most probable that research in the field will be both qualitative and quantitative for many years to come, in part because so many forms of serious leisure have still not been explored and in part because many leisure studies researchers either feel uncomfortable using exploratory methods or are opposed to them on scientific grounds.

I hope that it is clear in what has just been said that I am not indiscriminately championing qualitative-exploratory research over its counterpart, quantitative-confirmatory research. In my mind, it takes both to make a mature science. Exploration is, nevertheless, the most efficient and effective way to get to know an unknown area of social life, as the study of serious leisure was in its early years. But as I have indicated elsewhere (Stebbins, 1992b; 1997d), exploration is a long process, consisting of a number of concatenated, detailed studies that together lead to a substantial and valid grounded theory. A single study of, say, theatre people, is but a decent start toward a grounded theory of that form of leisure. It is a weaker start toward a theory of amateur art and an even weaker start toward a theory of amateurs in general or of all of serious leisure.

But, as just noted, there is still important scientific work to be done once a reasonably solid grounded theory has been constructed. Some researchers at this stage of knowledge have preferred to limit themselves to hypothetical questions, while others, having an interest in a heretofore unexplored area, have first explored it and then set about examining certain hypotheses, reporting the fruits of both phases in the same write-up (e.g., Yoder, 1997). Either approach can work well, so long as crucial personal and social elements of the leisure activity under study are not inadvertently overlooked because the researcher is too narrowly focussed. In some areas of serious leisure, mainly amateurism, collecting, and the competitive rule-based hobbies, I believe we now know enough to obviate such oversights.

Whatever the individual scholar's research approach, much work remains to be done in the realm of serious leisure. Moreover, there is no time to waste in accomplishing it, for the Information Age is upon us, and I am convinced that this kind of leisure offers a real and attractive, albeit nonremunerative, alternative to a life of full employment or one filled with extensive boredom when sufficient employment is unavailable.

Endnotes

Chapter 1

1. I am indebted to Stanley Parker for calling my attention to this possibility.

2. Readers familiar with earlier versions of this list of benefits will note that, here, I have changed the definition of self-gratification. The reason for this change is explained later in this chapter when self-gratification is discussed as one of the ten rewards of serious leisure.

3. Earlier written versions of this reward stressed its fun, enjoyable, even hedonistic side. More recently, however, it has become evident that satisfaction, as opposed to enjoyment, is also a main part of this reward, sometimes even the major part of it.

4. On commitment also see Buchanan (1985) and Shamir (1988). On the investment of time and energy in leisure, see Kelly (1983, pp. 195-196).

5. As good a descriptor as this is, Goffman's (1963:, pp. 143-45) decision to classify the quietly disaffiliated as deviant fails to square with the amateurs' views of themselves and, for that matter, with the canons of deviance theory (e.g., Stebbins, 1996, pp. 2-7).

6. Some fields of career volunteering, rooted as they are in altruistic ideals, may be shown in future research to be blessed with a higher degree of community-wide support than is available for amateur and hobbyist activities. My study of francophone volunteers reveals that they enjoy considerable support and respect in their linguistic community.

7. Rosenthal's (1981) study of chiropractors exemplifies this possibility.

8. This is an accurate portrayal of the concept of workaholic as originally set out by Machlowitz (1980). Perhaps because of the label itself, misinterpretations of her ideas have resulted in the popular notion that such people are driven obsessives.

Chapter 2

1. The intellectually oriented followers of politics, although they may be committed to certain political parties or doctrines, nonetheless spend significant amounts of time (and possibly money) informing themselves in this area. To be a hobbyist here, a person must pursue knowledge and understanding; he or she must do more than merely proclaim however fervently such and such a political stripe.

2. Over the years I have argued that an "intellectual relationship" exists between amateurs and professionals in that the former can maintain a broader knowledge of their activity than can most of the latter (Stebbins, 1992, p. 39). In this conceptualization, knowledge and the amateur activity guided by it are seen as parts of the same leisure pursuit. It now appears that it may be more accurate theoretically and empirically to classify the pursuit of a broad body of knowledge as a separate and distinctive liberal arts hobby which, however, some people may try to coordinate with a particular amateur or hobbyist activity.

3. On the question of the flexibility of hobbyist leisure and the social isolation of participants in certain types of it, see Olmsted (1993, pp. 30-31).

4. It appears that after seeing to basic needs nearly all remaining money is spent on the person's hobby. Such an orientation to leisure, however, is probably quite rare.

Chapter 3

1. Parker (1997) discusses "altruistic" and "cause-serving" volunteering as two separate types.

2. The classic study of altruistic volunteering is Titmuss's (1970) *The gift relationship*.

Chapter 4

1. It is possible, of course, that some participants once had a significant level of skill and training in the casual leisure in question, but these have atrophied to the point where they feel their participation is now more casual than serious.

2. This distinction between pleasurable/enjoyable and satisfying/ rewarding, although it appears to be valid in the commonsense world of leisure participants, goes unrecognized in the social psychology of leisure. In this field, enjoyment is regarded as one possible correlate of flow, well-being, or even leisure in general. See, for example, studies by Haworth and Hill (1992) and Haworth and Drucker (1991). Still, Mannell and Kleiber (1997, pp. 185-186) define satisfaction in much the same way as we do here. Moreover, they link it with rewards and motivation, as I did in chapter 1.

3. Just how much challenge - moderate or extreme - is required before flow is experienced is presently the subject of research. See Haworth and Evans (1995) for a review of the literature on this question.

4. Rojek's observation (1997, p. 392) that "leisure studies has turned a blind eye" to deviant leisure is most valid. His further observation that I "gloss" this question in Stebbins (1997a) (and therefore in this chapter) is also just, although it should be noted that elsewhere I examine in considerable depth several kinds of deviant leisure (see Stebbins, 1996d).

Chapter 5

1. Of course, there are hobbyist spectators of sport, people who spend considerable time each season following the sport in most, if not all, of its myriad details.

2. It is possible that small numbers of amateur scientists, for example mineralogists, ornithologists, and entomologists, also expand the scope of their serious leisure by touring.

3. The cultural dabbler may also be, or become, a mass tourist. Alternatively, he or she may be discouraged enough with tourism in general to give it up altogether.

4. I am speaking here of the late twentieth century. The most celebrated precursor of modern-day cultural tourism was the Grand Tour of the seventeenth and eighteenth centuries. Nonetheless, it was much more exclusive than contemporary cultural tourism, designed as it was for the education, edification, and personality development of upper-class English gentlemen (see, Hudson, 1993).

5. The less likely cultural tourists are to venture outside their environmental bubble, the more likely they are to value the practical information contained in these guides (Greenblat & Gagnon, 1983, p. 104)

Chapter 6

1. The first study consisted of 88 cases of selfishness reported by 67 student respondents in an upperdivision sociology course. The data were gathered in 1980. For further details about the study, see Stebbins (1993b). Twenty-five adult amateur baseball players were interviewed in the second study (see Stebbins, 1979).

Chapter 7

1. The fourth function, which is vocational, is the only one that falls completely

outside the domain of leisure.

Chapter 8

1. Unique ethos was the only quality not correlated.

2. Following Unruh (1979, pp. 116-118), "strangers" in leisure social worlds can be defined as intermediaries who normally participate little in the leisure activity itself, but who nonetheless do something important to enable it to happen.

3. Professionals are found in some of the crafts, particularly those using clay, glass, and metal, which is why I described craft work as amateur *and* hobbyist activity in *After Work* (Stebbins, 1998a).

4. A number of these conditions are discussed in Stebbins (1992a, pp. 71-77).

5. My classification here of genealogy, or family history, as a liberal arts hobby contradicts my earlier classification of it as an amateur science (see Stebbins, 1998a, p. 45). Lambert's work, which I read subsequently, has convinced me that no real professional counterpart of the family historian exists, notwithstanding the availability of commercial genealogical services in every large city. I understand these services to be enterprises run by business people rather than by professionals, as the latter are sociologically defined in chapter 2. For definitions of genealogy and family history, see Lambert (1996b, p. 116).

6. I am paraphrasing David Smith (1997) here, who defines "grassroots associations" as local, formal and semiformal organizations which are commonly composed purely of volunteers and which he contrasts with "volunteer programs," as these are created and run by work organizations.

7. All the articles composing this special issue are briefly summarized here, with the exception of Parker's (Parker, 1997). It is discussed at various points in chapter 3.

Chapter 9

1. The term "formal retirement" refers to the end of a lifetime of work as enforced by a law, pension plan, organizational policy, or similar constraint. Nevertheless, it is obvious that, beyond this juncture, these constraints fail to prevent a person from taking up certain kinds of remunerated work.

2. The term "First World" refers to the developed nations outside the former Communist bloc nations, which make up the Second World.

Chapter 10

1. This practice of mandatory overtime for existing employees is said to cost the employer significantly less than hiring additional full-time employees to perform the overtime tasks. For instance, management economizes by avoiding the costs of fringe benefits they would have to grant to new personnel.

2. These authors are by no means the first analysts to note these trends. For example, Jenkins and Sherman (1979) discussed them from a British standpoint, and three years later Jones (1982) described the same processes at work in Australia. Nevertheless, Rifkin (1995, p. 6) was able to observe that the enormous corporate spending on electronic technology during the 1980s began to pay off only in the early 1990s through increased productivity, reduced labor costs, and greater profits. The cost of labor is being reduced chiefly by shrinking the workforce.

3. See, for example, Jenkins and Sherman (1981) and Sherman (1986). Rifkin comes closer than the others to completing the story when he examines the role of volunteers and community service in the closing chapters of his book.

4. Unruh's (1979) concept of the social world resembles in many ways Maffesoli's (1996) concept of the tribe.

Chapter 11

1. The only exception of which I am aware is found in Israel, where leisure education is now part of the secondary school curriculum. Serious leisure serves as the theoretical foundation for teaching in this area.

2. Mason-Mullet, apparently unaware of the small literature on volunteering as leisure (see chapter 3), organizes her discussion around what she sees as the novel idea that, when done as participative citizenship, volunteering is in reality leisure.

3. This is not to exclude the Third World from eventually being compared as well. But considerable ethnographic work on serious leisure must first be done there before meaningful cross-national comparisons involving these countries can be carried out. A basic corpus of ethnographic research of this sort now exists for the West, even if most of it has been conducted in North America.

4. A validity check could be effected by asking a small sample of, say, five participants in a given serious leisure activity to read the ethnographic portions of research previously conducted on it (such material is usually readable by nonprofessionals). Thus, a sample of amateur mycologists in say two or three European countries could be asked to comment on the validity for them of the ethnographic passages in Gary Fine's articles, which report his observations on American mushroom collectors (e.g., Fine, 1988).

5. On the role of exploration in the leisure sciences, see Stebbins (1997d).

Bibliography

Ainley, M. G. (1980). The contribution of the amateur to North American ornithology: A historical perspective. *Living Bird*, 18, 161-177.

Altheide, D.L., & Snow, R.P. (1991). *Media worlds in the postjournalism era.* Hawthorne, NY: Aldine de Gruyter.

American Association for Retired Persons (1988). *Attitudes of Americans over 45 years of age on volunteerism.* Washington, D.C.

Apostle, R. (1992). Curling for cash: The "professionalization" of a popular Canadian sport. *Culture*, 12 (2), 17-28.

Arai, S.M. (1997). Volunteers within a changing society: The uses of empowerment theory in understanding serious leisure. *World Leisure & Recreation*, 39 (3), 19-22.

Arai, S.M. (in press). A typology of volunteers for a changing sociopolitical context: The impact on social capital, citizenship, and civil society. *Loisir et Société/Society and Leisure.*

Arai, S.M., & Pedlar, A.M. (1997). Building Communities through leisure: Citizen participation in a healthy communities initiative. *Journal of Leisure Research*, 29, 167-182.

Argyle, M. (1992). *The social psychology of everyday life.* New York, NY: Routledge.

Aronowitz, S., & DiFazio, W. (1994). *The jobless future: Sci-tech and the dogma of work.* Minneapolis, MN: University of Minnesota Press.

Baldwin, C.K., & Norris, P.A. (1999). Exploring the dimensions of serious leisure: "Love me - love my dog." *Journal of Leisure Research*, 31, 1-17.

Benoit, J., & Perkins, K.B. (1997). Volunteer fire fighting activity in North America as serious leisure. *World Leisure & recreation*, 39 (3), 23-29.

Bishop, J., & Hoggett, P. (1986). *Organizing around enthusiasms: Mutual aid in leisure.* London, Eng.: Comedia Publishing Group.

Blacksell, S., & Phillips, D.R. (1994). *Paid to volunteer: The extent of paying volunteers in the 1990s*. London, Eng.: The Volunteer Centre UK.

Blumer, H. (1968). *Symbolic interactionism*. Englewood Cliffs, NJ: Prentice-Hall.

Bonjean, C.M., Markham, W.T., & Macken, P.O. (1994). Measuring self-expression in volunteer organizations: A theory-level questionnaire. *Journal of Applied Behavioral Science*, 30, 487-515.

Bosse, R., & Ekerdt, D. J. (1981). Change in self-perception of leisure activities with retirement. *The Gerontologist*, 21, 650-654.

Bosserman, P. (1993). The leisure framework. In M. Kaplan (Ed.), *Barbershopping: Musical and social harmony* (pp. 73-94). Madison, NJ: Fairleigh Dickinson University Press.

Bosserman, P., & Gagan, R. (1972). Leisure and voluntary action. In D.H. Smith (Ed.), *Voluntary action research: 1972*. Lexington, MA.: D.C. Heath.

Boulding, K. (1973). *The economy of love and fear*. Belmont, CA: Wadsworth.

Branden, N. (1961). Isn't everyone selfish? In A. Rand (Ed.), *The virtue of selfishness*. New York, NY: New American Library.

Brightbill, C.K. (1961). *Man and leisure: A philosophy of recreation*. Englewood Cliffs, NJ: Prentice-Hall.

Brockett, R.G., & Darkenwald, G.G. (1987). Trends in research on the adult learner. In R.G. Brockett (Ed.), *Continuing education in the year 2000* (pp. 29-40). San Francisco, CA: Jossey-Bass.

Buchanan, T. (1985). Commitment and leisure behavior. *Leisure Sciences*, 7, 401-420.

Burdge, R.J. (1989). The evolution of leisure and recreation research from multidisciplinarity to interdisciplinarity. In E.L. Jackson & T.L. Burton (Eds.), *Understanding leisure and recreation* (pp. 29-46). State College, PA: Venture.

Carp, F.M. (1968). Differences among older workers, volunteers, and persons who are neither. *Journal of Gerontology*, 23, 497-501.

Carpenter, G., Patterson, I., & Pritchard, M. (1990). An investigation of the relationship between freedom in Leisure and self-directed learning. *Schole*, 5, 53-66.

Chambré, S.M. (1987). *Good deeds in old age: Volunteering by the new leisure class*. Lexington, MA: Lexington Books.

Chaplin, D. (1999). Consuming work/productive leisure: The consumption patterns of second home environments. *Leisure Studies*, 18, 41-56.

Clark, A. (1997, September 20). Comedy college. *Financial Post*, p. 36.

Codina, N. (1999). Tendencias emergentes en el comportamiento de ocio: El ocio serio y su evaluación. *Revista de Psicología Social*, 14, 331-346.

Cohen, E. (1972). Toward a sociology of international tourism. *Social Research*, 39, 164-182.

Cohen, E. (1974). Who is a tourist? A conceptual clarification. *Sociological Review*, 22, 527-555.

Cohen, E. (1984). The sociology of tourism: Approaches, issues, and findings. In R.H. Turner & J.F. Short, Jr. (Eds.), *Annual Review of Sociology*, Vol. 10 (pp. 373-392). Palo Alto, CA: Annual Reviews Inc.

Cole, S. (1997). Book fans brought together by clubs. *Calgary Herald*, Sunday, 7 September, p. E2.

Cooley, C.H. (1922). *Human nature and the social order* (rev. ed.). New York, NY: Charles Scribner's Sons.

Crouch, D. (1993). Commitment, enthusiasms and creativity in the world of allotment holding. *World Leisure & Recreation*, 35 (spring), 19-22.

Crouch, D., & Ward, C. (1994). *The allotment: Its landscape and culture*. Nottingham, Eng.: Mushroom Bookshop.

Csikszentmihalyi, M. (1975). *Beyond boredom and anxiety*. San Francisco, CA: Jossey-Bass.

Csikszentmihalyi, M. (1990). *Flow: The psychology of optimal experience*. New York, NY: Harper & Row.

Csikszentmihalyi, M., & LeFevre, J. (1989). Optimal experience in work and leisure. *Journal of Personality and Social Psychology*, 56, 815-822.

Cuskelly, G., & Harrington, M. (1997). Volunteers and leisure: Evidence of marginal and career volunteerism in sport. *World Leisure & Recreation*, 39 (3), 11-18.

Dannefer, D. (1980). Rationality and passion in private experience: Modern consciousness and the social world of old-car collectors. *Social Problems*, 27, 392-412.

DeBono, E. (1967). *New think: The use of lateral thinking*. New York, NY: Basic Books.

Delbaere, R. (1994). Le tourisme culturel et récréotouristique, leurs approches méthodologiques et leurs potentialités. Paper presented at the International Leisure Studies Conference, Université du Québec à Trois-Rivières, Trois-Rivières, Québec, 3-4 November.

Deshler, D. (1994). Participation motivation in adult education. In T. Husén & T.N. Postlethwaite (Eds.), *The international encylopedia of education* (2nd ed.), Vol 10

174

(pp. 4325-4330). Tarrytown, NY: Elsevier Science.

Deveraux, M. 1985. *One in every five: A survey of adult education in Canada.* Ottawa, ON: Statistics Canada and Department of Secretary of State.

de Vroom, B., & Blomsma, M. (1991). The Netherlands: An extreme case. In M. Kohli, M. Rein, A.-M. Guillemard, & H. van Gunsteren (Eds.), *Time for retirement: Comparative studies of early exit from the labor force* (pp. 97-126). Cambridge, Eng.: Cambridge University Press.

Dickson, A. (1974). Preface. In D.H. Smith (Ed.), *Voluntary action research: 1974.* Lexington, MA: D.C. Heath.

Downie, R.S., & Telfer, E. (1969). *Respect for persons.* London, Eng.: George Allen & Unwin.

Driver, B.L. (Ed.) (1970). *Elements of Outdoor Recreation Planning.* Ann Arbor, MI: University of Michigan Press.

Dubin, R. (1992). *Central life interests: Creative individualism in a complex world.* New Brunswick, NJ: Transaction.

Duke, C. (1994). Adult and continuing education. In T. Husén & T.N. Postlethwaite (Eds.), *The international encyclopedia of education* (2nd ed.) Vol. 1 (pp. 89-94). Tarrytown, NY: Elsevier Science.

Ellis, J.R. (1993). Volunteerism as an enhancement to career   development. *Journal of Employment Conselling,* 30, 127-132.

Etheridge, M., & Neapolitan, J. (1985). Amateur craft-workers: Marginal roles in a marginal art world. *Sociological Spectrum,* 5, 53-76.

Faché, W. (1998). Leren voor de vrije tijd en leren als vrijetijdsbesteding. In J. Katus, J.W.M. Kessels, and P.E. Schedler (Eds.), *Andragologie in transformatie.* Amsterdam: Boom.

Fain, G.S. (1991). Moral leisure. In G.S. Fain (Ed.), *Leisure and ethics: Reflections on the philosophy of leisure,* Vol. 1 (pp. 7-30). Reston, VA: American Alliance for Health, Physical Education, Recreation and Dance.

Federico, R. (1983). The decision to end a performing career in ballet. In J.B. Kamerman & R. Martorella (Eds.), *Performers and performances: The social organization of artistic work* (pp. 57-70). New York, NY: Praeger.

Fine, G.A. (1987). Community and boundary: Personal experience stories of mushroom collectors. *Journal of Folklore Research,* 24, 223-240.

Fine, G.A. (1988). Dying for a Laugh. *Western Folklore,* 47, 77-194.

Fine, G.A. (1989). Mobilizing fun: Provisioning resources in leisure worlds. *Sociology of Sport Journal,* 6, 319-34.

Fine, G.A., & Holyfield, L. (1996). Trusting fellows: Secrecy, trust, and voluntary allegiance in leisure spheres. *Social Psychological Quarterly*, 59, 22-38.

Finnegan, R. (1989). *The hidden musicians: Music-making in an English town.* Cambridge, Eng.: Cambridge University Press.

Fischer, L. R., Mueller, D. P., & Cooper, P. W. (1991). Old volunteers: A discussion of the Minnesota Senior Study. *The Gerontologist*, 31, 183-194.

Fischer, L.R., & Schaffer, K.B. (1993). *Older volunteers: A guide to research and practice*. Newbury Park, CA: Sage.

Freidson, E. (1978). The official construction of occupations: An essay on the practical epistemology of work. Paper presented at the 9th World Congress of Sociology, Uppsala, Sweden, August.

Floro, G.K. (1978). What to look for in a study of the volunteer in the work world. In R.P. Wolensky & E.J. Miller (Eds.), *The small city and regional community* (pp. 194-202). Stevens Point, WI: Foundation Press.

Fodor Travel Publications (1994). *Fodor's great American learning vacations*. New York, NY: Fodor Travel Publications.

Gates, J.T. (1991). Music participation: Theory, research, and policy. *Bulletin of the Council for Research in Music Education*, no. 109 (Summer).

Gelber, S.M. (1992). Free market metaphor: The historical dynamics of stamp collecting. *Comparative Studies in Society and History*, 34 (4), 742-769.

Gelber, S.M. (1997). Do-it yourself: Constructing, repairing and maintaining domestic masculinity. *American Quarterly*, 49 (1), 66-112.

Gibson, H. (1998). Active sport tourism: Who participates? *Leisure Studies*, 17, 155-170.

Glaser, B.G., & A.L. Strauss (1967). *The Discovery of Grounded Theory*, Chicago, IL: Aldine.

Glyptis, S. (1989). *Leisure and unemployment*. Milton Keynes, Eng.: Open University Press.

Godbey, G. (1990). *Leisure in your life: An exploration* (3rd ed.). State College, PA: Venture.

Goff, S.J., Fick, D.S., & Oppliger, R.A. (1997). The moderating effect of spouse support on the relation between serious leisure and spouses' perceived leisure-family conflict. *Journal of Leisure Research*, 29, 47-60.

Goffman, E. (1961). *Asylums: Essays on the social situation of mental patients and other inmates*. Garden City, NY: Doubleday.

Goffman, E. (1963). *Stigma: Notes on the management of spoiled identity.* Englewood Cliffs, NJ: Prentice-Hall.

Greenblat, C.S., & Gagnon, J.H. (1983). Temporary strangers: Travel and tourism from a sociological perspective. *Sociological Perspectives*, 26, 89-110.

Gross, R. (1977). *A Handbook for the Lifelong Learner.* New York, NY: Simon and Schuster.

Gross, R. (1982). *The independent scholar's handbook.* Reading, MA: Addison-Wesley.

Hall, C. M. (1992). Review. Adventure, sport and health tourism. In B. Weiler & C. M. Hall (Eds.), *Special interest tourism* (pp. 141-158). New York, NY: Wiley.

Hall, C. M, & Weiler, B. (1992). Introduction. What's special about special interest tourism. In B. Weiler & C.M. Hall (Eds.), *Special interest tourism* (pp. 1-14). New York, NY: Wiley.

Hall, P.M. (1987). Interactionism and the study of social organization. *The Sociological Quarterly*, 28, 1-22.

Hamilton-Smith, E. (1971). The preparation of volunteer workers with adolescent groups. *Australian Social Work*, 24 (3 & 4), 26-33.

Hamilton-Smith, E. (1992). Work, leisure and optimal experience. *Leisure Studies*, 11, 243-256.

Hamilton-Smith, E. (1993). In the Australian bush: Some reflections on serious leisure. *World Leisure & Recreation*, 35 (1), 10-13.

Hamilton-Smith, E. (1995). The connexions of scholarship. *Newsletter* (Official newsletter of RC13 of the International Sociological Association), March: 4-9.

Harries, G.D., & Currie, R.R. (1998). Cognitive dissonance: A consequence of serious leisure. *World Leisure & Recreation*, 40 (3), 36-41.

Hastings, D.W., Kurth, S.B., & Schloder, M. (1996). Work routines in the serious leisure career of Canadian and U.S. masters swimmers. *Avanté*, 2, 73-92.

Hastings, D.W., Kurth, S.B., Schloder, M., & Cyr, Darrell (1995). Reasons for participating in a serious leisure: Comparison of Canadian and U.S. masters swimmers. *International Review for Sociology of Sport* 30, 101-119.

Haworth, J.T. (1986). Meaningful activity and psychological models of non-employment. *Leisure Studies*, 5, 281-297.

Haworth, J.T. (1994). Environmental categories of experience and well-being: The importance of leisure. *World Leisure & Recreation*, 36 (4), 10-14.

Haworth, J.T. (1997). *Work, leisure and well-being.* London, Eng.: Routledge.

Haworth, J.T., & Drucker, J. (1991). Psychological well-being and access to categories of experience in unemployed young adults. *Leisure Studies*, 10, 265-274.

Haworth, J.T., & Evans, S. (1995). Challenge, skill and positive subjective states in the daily life of a sample of YTS students. *Journal of Occupational and Organizational Psychology*, 68, 109-121.

Haworth, J.T., & Hill, S. (1992). Work. leisure, and psychological well-being in a sample of young adults. *Journal of Community & Applied Social Psychology*, 2, 147-160.

Hearn, H.L. (1972). Aging and the artistic career. *The Gerontologist*, 12, 357-362.

Hemingway, J. (1995). Leisure studies and interpretive social inquiry. *Leisure Studies*, 14, 32-47.

Henderson, K.A. (1981). Motivations and perceptions of volunteerism as a leisure activity. *Journal of Leisure Research*, 13, 208-218.

Henderson, K.A. (1984). Volunteerism as leisure. *Journal of Voluntary Action Research*, 13, 55-63.

Henderson, K.A., Bedini, L., Hecht, L., & Schuler, R. (1995). Women with physical disabilities and the negotiation of leisure constraints. Leisure Studies, 14, 17-31.

Hewitt, J.P. (1991). *Self and society* (5th ed). Boston, MA: Allyn and Bacon.

Hodgkinson, V.A., & Weitzman, M.A. (1992). *Giving and volunteering in the United States: Findings from a national survey*. Washington, DC: Independent Sector.

Houle, C.O. (1961). *The inquiring mind*. Madison, WI: University of Wisconsin Press.

Howard, A. (Ed.). (1995). *The changing nature of work*. San Francisco, CA: Jossey-Bass.

Howe, C. (1995). Factors impacting leisure in middle-aged adults throughout the world: United States. *World Leisure & Recreation*, 37 (1), 37-38.

Hudson, R. (Ed.) (1993). *The grand tour 1592-1796*. London, Eng.: The Folio Society.

Independent Sector (1988). *Giving and volunteering in the United States: Findings from a national survey*. Washington, D.C.

Iso-Ahola, S.E. (1989). Motivation for leisure. In E.L. Jackson & T.L. Burton (Eds.), *Understanding leisure and recreation* (pp. 247-280). State College, PA: Venture.

Jackson, E.L., & Burton, T.L. (1989). Mapping the past. In E.L. Jackson & T.L. Burton (Eds.), *Understanding leisure and recreation* (pp. 3-28). State College, PA: Venture.

Jahoda, M. (1979). The impact of unemployment in the 1930s and the 1970s. *Bulletin of the British Psychological Society*, 32, 309-314.

Jarvis, N., & King, L. (1997). Volunteers in uniformed youth organizations. *World Leisure & Recreation*, 39 (3), 6-10.

Jarvis, P. (1995). *Adult and continuing education* (2nd ed.). London, Eng.: Routledge.

Jenkins, C., & Sherman, B. (1979). *The Collapse of Work*. London, Eng.: Eyre Methuen.

Jenkins, C., & Sherman, B. (1981). *The Leisure Shock*. London, Eng.: Eyre Methuen.

Jenner, J.R. (1982). Participation, leadership, and the role of volunteerism among selected women volunteers. *Journal of Voluntary Action Research*, 11, 27-38.

Jones, B. (1982). *Sleepers wake! Technology and the future of work*. Melbourne, Austalia.: Oxford University Press.

Jung, B. (1996). Poland. In G. Cushman, A.J. Veal, & J. Zuzanek (Eds.), *World leisure participation: Free time in the global village* (pp. 183-198). Wallingford, Oxon, U.K.: CAB International.

Juniu, S., Tedrick, T., & Boyd, R. (1996). Leisure or work? Amateur and professional musicians' perception of rehearsal and performance. *Journal of Leisure Research*, 28, 44-56.

Kaplan, M. (1960). *Leisure in America: A social inquiry*. New York, NY: Wiley.

Kaplan, M. (1975). *Leisure: Theory and policy*. New York, NY: Wiley.

Katz, J. (1988). *Seductions of crime: Moral and sensual attractions of doing evil*. New York, NY: Basic Books.

Kay, T. 1990. Active unemployment - A leisure pattern for the future. *Loisir et Société/Society and Leisure*, 12, 413-430.

Kelly, J.R. (1983). *Leisure identities and interactions*. Boston, MA: George Allen & Unwin.

Kelly, J.R. (1990). Leisure (2nd ed.). Englewood Cliffs, NJ: Prentice-Hall.

Kelly, J.R. (1997). Activity and ageing: Challenge in retirement. In J.T. Haworth (Ed.), *Work, leisure and well-being* (pp. 165-179). London, Eng.: Routledge.

Kelly, J.R., & Godbey, G. (1992). *The Sociology of Leisure*. State College, PA: Venture.

King, F.L. (1997). *Why contemporary Texas women quilt: A link to the sociology of leisure*. Unpublished doctoral dissertation, Unviersity of Texas, Arlington.

Kleiber, D.A. (1996) (July). Personal expressiveness and the transcendence of negative life events. Paper presented at the 4th World Congress of Leisure Research, World Leisure and Recreation Association, Cardiff, Wales.

Knowles, M.S. (1975). *Self-directed learning*, New York, NY: Association Press.

Knowles, M.S. (1980). *The modern practice of adult education* (rev. ed). Chicago, IL: Chicago Association Press.

Krippendorf, J. (1986). The new tourist - Turning point for leisure and travel. *Tourism Management*, 7, 131-135.

Lambert, R.D. (1995a). Looking for genealogical motivation. *Families*, 34, 73-80.

Lambert, R.D. (1995b). Becoming a family historian. *Families*, 34, 223-232.

Lambert, R.D. (1996a). Doing family history. *Families*, 35, 11-25.

Lambert, R.D. (1996b). The family historian and temporal orientations towards the ancestral past. *Time & Society*, 5, 115-143.

Lambing, M.L.B. (1972). Leisure-time pursuits among retired blacks by social status. *The Gerontologist*, 12, 363-367.

Lankford, J. (1981a). Amateurs and astrophysics: A neglected aspect of the development of a scientific speciality. *Social Studies of Science*, 11, 275-303.

Lankford, J. (1981b). Amateurs versus professionals: The controversy over telescope size in late Victorian science. *Isis*, 72, 11-28.

Laverie, D.A. (1998). Motivations for ongoing participation in a fitness activity. *Leisure Sciences*, 20, 277-302.

Lee, Y., Dattilo, J., & Howard, D. (1994). The complex and dynamic nature of leisure experience. *Journal of Leisure Research*, 26, 195-211.

Lefkowitz, B. (1979). *Breaktime*. New York, NY: Penguin.

Lewis, L.S., & Brissett, D. (1981). Paradise on demand. *Society*, 18 (July/August), 85-90.

Lindesmith, A.R., Strauss, A.L., & Denzin, N.K. (1991). *Social psychology* (7th ed). Englewood Cliffs, NJ: Prentice-Hall.

Litner, M. (1992). Ethics and leisure: An essential component of a leisure education course. *Leisure Information Quarterly*, 18 (no. 4), 1-2.

Lobo, F., & Watkins, G. (1995). Mature-aged unemployment and leisure. *World Leisure & Recreation*, 36 (4), 22-28.

MacCannell, D. (1976). *The tourist: A new theory of the leisure class*. New York, NY: Schocken Books.

Machlowitz. M. (1980). *Workaholics: Living with them, working with them*. Reading, MA: Addison-Wesley.

Maffesoli, M. (1996). *The time of the tribes: The decline of individualism in mass society*. London, Eng.: Sage.

Maines, D.R. (1982). In search of mesostructure. *Urban Life*, 11, 267-279.

Mannell, R.C. (1993). High investment activity and life satisfaction among older adults: Overcoming psychological inertia through committed, serious leisure, and flow activites. In J.R. Kelly (Ed.), *Activity and aging: Staying involved in later life* (pp.125-145). Newbury Park, CA: Sage.

Mannell, R.C., & Kleiber, D.A. (1997). *A social psychology of leisure*. State College, PA: Venture.

Mason-Mullet, S. (1995). Education for leisure - Moving towards community. In G.S. Fain (Ed.), *Leisure and ethics: Reflections on the philosophy of leisure*, Vol. II (pp. 229-256). Reston, VA: American Association for Leisure and Recreation.

McDonald, P.L., & Wanner, R.A. (1990). *Retirement in Canada*.Toronto, ON: Butterworths Canada.

McGill, J. (1996). *Developing leisure identities: A pilot project*. Brampton, ON: Brampton Caledon Community Living.

McKim, J.B. (1997). Keeping the revolution alive. *Boston Globe*, Sunday, 29 June, B2.

McMillon, B. (1991). *Volunteer Vacations*. Chicago, IL: Chicago Review Press.

McPherson, B.D. (1990). *Aging as a social process* (2nd ed.). Toronto, ON: Butterworths Canada.

McQuarrie, F., & Jackson, E.L. (1996). Connections between negotiation of leisure constraints and serious leisure: An exploratory study of adult amateur ice skaters. *Loisir et Société/Society and Leisure*, 19, 459-483.

Mittelstaedt, R.D. (1990-91). The Civil War reenactment: A growing trend in creative leisure behavior. *Leisure Information Quarterly*, 17 (4), 4-6.

Mittelstaedt, R.D. (1995). Reenacting the American Civil War: A unique form of serious leisure for adults. *World Leisure & Recreation*, 37 (1), 23-27.

Mueller, M.W. (1975). Economic determinants of volunteer work by women. *Signs*, 1, 325-338.

Nash, D. (1981). Tourism as an anthropological subject. *Current Anthropology*, 22, 461-468.

Neulinger, J. (1974). *The psychology of leisure: Research approaches to the study of leisure*. Springfield, IL: Charles C. Thomas.

Neulinger, J. (1981). *To leisure: An introduction*. Boston, MA: Allyn and Bacon.

Nicols, G., & King. L. (1999). Redefining the recruitment niche for the Guide Association in the United Kingdom. *Leisure Sciences*, 21, 307-320.

Niyazi, F. (1996). *Volunteering by people with disabilities*. London, Eng.: National Centre for Volunteering.

Olmsted, A.D. (1988). Morally controversial leisure: The social world of the gun collector. *Symbolic Interaction*, 11, 277-287.

Olmsted, A.D. (1991). Collecting: Leisure investment or obsession? *Journal of Social Behavior and Personality*, 6, 287-306.

Olmsted, A.D. (1993). Hobbies and serious leisure. *World Leisure & Recreation*, 35 (Spring), 27-32.

Olmsted, A.D., & Horna, J.A. (1989). Pin collectors and others: Pin trading at the 1988 Calgary Winter Olympics. Paper presented at the annual meeting of the Popular Culture Association, St. Louis, MO.

Osgood, N.J. (1993). Creative activity and the arts: Possibilities and programs. In J.R. Kelly (Ed.), *Activity and aging: Staying involved in later life* (pp. 174-186). Newbury Park, CA: Sage.

Parker, S.R. (1987). Working for peace as serious leisure. *Leisure Information Quarterly*, 13 (no. 4), 9-10.

Parker, S.R. (1992). Volunteering as serious leisure. *Journal of Applied Recreation Research*, 17, 1-11.

Parker, S.R., editor, (1993). *World Leisure & Recreation* (special issue on serious leisure), 35 (Spring), 1-32.

Parker, S.R. (1994). Group life: Individual interests and social purposes. In *New routes for leisure: World leisure congress* (pp. 423-428). Lisbon, Portugal: Instituto de Ciencias Sociais, Universidade de Lisboa.

Parker, S.R. (1996). Serious leisure - A middle-class phenomenon? In M. Collins (Ed.), *Leisure in industrial and post-industrial societies* (pp. 327-332). Eastbourne, Eng.: Leisure Studies Association.

Parker, S.R. (1997). Volunteering - Altruism, markets, causes and leisure. *World Leisure & Recreation*, 39 (3), 4-5.

Parker, S.R., Hamilton-Smith, E., & Davidson, P. (1993). Serious and other leisure: Thirty Australians. *World Leisure & Recreation*, 35 (Spring), 14-18.

Parnes, H., Crowley, J.E., Haurin, R.J., Less, L.J., Morgan, W.R., Mott, F.L., &

Nestel, G. (1985). *Retirement among American men.* Lexington, MA: D.C. Heath.

Parsons, T. (1940). Motivation of economic activities. *Canadian Journal of Economics and Political Science*, 6, 187-203.

Partington, J.T. (1995). *Making music.* Ottawa, ON: Carleton University Press.

Patterson, I. (1997). Serious leisure as an alternative to a work career for people with disabilities. *Australian Disability Review*, 2, 20-27.

Pearce, J.L. (1993). *Volunteers: The organizational behavior of unpaid workers.* New York, NY: Routledge.

Pieper, J. (1963). *Leisure: The basis of culture*, trans. by A. Dru. New York, NY: New American Library.

Plog, S.C. (1991). *Leisure travel: Making it a growth market. . . again!* New York, NY: Wiley.

Prost, A. (1992). Leisure and disability: A contradiction in terms. *World Leisure & Recreation*, 34 (3), 8-9.

Raisborough, J. (1999). Research note: The concept of serious leisure and women's experiences of the Sea Cadet Corps. *Leisure Studies*, 18, 67-72.

Rand, A. (1961). *The virtue of selfishness.* New York, NY: New American Library.

Reid, D.G. (1995). *Work and leisure in the 21st century: From production to citizenship.* Toronto, ON: Wall & Emerson.

Reisinger, Y. (1994). Tourist - host contact as a part of cultural tourism. *World Leisure & Recreation*, 36 (Summer), 24-28.

Richards, G. (1996). The transatlantic vacation divide: A question of time? Paper presented at the New Strategies for Everyday Life conference, December, Tilburg, the Netherlands.

Riedler, M. (1992). *Barbershop: Musikalische und soziale aspekte eines kulturellen phanomens im angelsachesischen raum.* Vienna, Austria: Hochschule fur Musik und darstellende Kunst, Diplomarbeit.

Rifkin, J. (1995). *The end of work: The decline of the global labor force and the dawn of the post-market era.* New York, NY: G.P. Putnam's Sons.

Roadburg, A. (1985). *Aging: Retirement, leisure, and work in Canada.* Toronto, ON: Methuen.

Roberts, K. (1994). Untying leisure's conceptual knot: Returning to a residual time definition. *Newsletter* (Research Committee 13 of the International Sociological Association), November, 3-9.

Robinson, J.P., & Godbey G. (1997). *Time for life: The surprising ways Americans*

183

use their time. University Park, PA: Pennsylvania State University Press.

Rojek, C. (1995). *Decentring leisure: Rethinking leisure theory*. London, Eng.: Sage.

Rojek, C. (1997). Leisure theory: Retrospect and prospect. *Loisir et Société/Society and Leisure*, 20, 383-400.

Rosenthal, S.F. (1981). Marginal or mainstream: Two studies of contemporary chiropractic. *Sociological Focus*, 14, 271-285.

Ross, D.P. (1990). Economic dimensions of volunteer work in Canada. Ottawa, ON: Department of the Secretary of State, Government of Canada.

Rothenberg, M. (1981). Organization and control: Professionals and amateurs in American astronomy. *Social Studies of Science*, 11, 305-325.

Samuel, N. (1994a). In *New Routes for Leisure* (pp. 45-57). Lisbon, Portugal: Instituto de Ciências Sociais, Universidade de Lisboa.

Samuel, N. (1994b). Unemployment and leisure. *World Leisure & Recreation*, 36 (4), 5-9.

Schellenberg, G. (1994). *The road to retirement: Demographic and economic changes in the 1990s*. Ottawa, On: Candian Council on Social Development.

Schor, J.B. (1991). *The overworked American: The unexpected Decline of leisure*. New York, NY: Basic Books.

Scott, D., & Godbey, G.C. (1992). An analysis of adult play groups: Social versus serious participation in contract bridge. *Leisure Sciences*, 14, 47-67.

Scott, D., & Godbey, G.C. (1994). Recreation specializaiton in the social world of contract bridge. *Journal of Leisure Research*, 26, 275-295.

Scott, S. (1993). Local hero: Metis history fills cupboards, head and heart. *Calgary Herald Neighbors*, (17-23 November).

Selman, G., Cooke, M., Selman, M., & Dampier, P. (1998). *The foundations of adult education in Canada* (2nd ed.). Toronto, ON: Thompson Educational Publishing.

Shamir, B. (1985). Unemployment and "free time" - The role of the Protestant ethic and work involvement. *Leisure Studies*, 4, 333-345.

Shamir, B. (1988). Commitment and leisure. *Sociological Perspectives*, 31, 238-258.

Shamir, B. (1992). Some correlates of leisure identity salience: Three exploratory studies. *Journal of Leisure Research*, 24, 301-323.

Sheppard, H. L. (1976). Work and retirement. In R. Binstock & E. Shanas (Eds.), *Handbook of aging and the social sciences* (pp. 286-309). New York, NY: Van Nostrand Reinhold.

Shorman, B. (1966). Working at leisure. London, Eng.: Methuen London Ltd.

Siegenthaler, K.L., & Gonsalez, G.L. (1997). Youth sports as serious leisure: A critique. *Journal of Sport and Social Issues*, 21, 298-314.

Siegenthaler, K.L., & Lam, T.C.M. (1992). Commitment and ego-involvement in recreational tennis. *Leisure Studies*, 14, 303-315.

Simmel, G. (1949). The sociology of sociability. *American Journal of Sociology*, 55, 254-261.

Smith, D.H. (1975). Voluntary action and voluntary groups. In A. Inkeles, J. Coleman, & N. Smelser (Eds.), *Annual Review of Sociology*, vol. 1. Palo Alto, CA: Annual Reviews Inc.

Smith, D.H. (1981). Altruism, volunteers, and volunteerism. *Journal of Voluntary Action Research*, 10, 21-36.

Smith, D.H. (1997). The rest of the nonprofit sector: Grassroots associations as the dark matter ignored in prevailing "flat earth" maps of the sector. *Nonprofit and Voluntary Sector Quarterly*, 26, 114-131.

Stebbins, R.A. (1970). Career: The subjective approach. *The Sociological Quarterly*, 11, 32-49.

Stebbins, R.A. (1978). Amateurism and postretirement years. *Journal of Physical Education and Recreation* (*Leisure Today* supplement), 49 (October), 40-41.

Stebbins, R.A. (1979). *Amateurs: On the margin between work and leisure*. Beverly Hills, CA: Sage.

Stebbins, R.A. (1980a). "Amateur" and "hobbyist" as concepts for the study of leisure problems. *Social Problems*, 27, 413-417.

Stebbins, R.A. (1980b). Avocational science: The amateur routine in archaeology and astronomy, *International Journal of Comparative Sociology*, 21, 34-48.

Stebbins, R.A. (1981). Toward a social psychology of stage fright. In M. Hart & S. Birrell (Eds.), *Sport in the sociocultural process* (pp. 156-163). Dubuque, IA: W.C. Brown.

Stebbins, R.A. (1982). Serious leisure: a conceptual statement. *Pacific Sociological Review*, 25, 251-272.

Stebbins, R.A. (1990). *The laugh-makers: Stand-up comedy as art, business, and life-style*. Montréal, QC and Kingston, ON: McGill-Queen's University Press.

Stebbins, R.A. (1992a). *Amateurs, professionals, and serious leisure*. Montreal, QC and Kingston, ON: McGill-Queen's University Press.

Stebbins, R.A. (1992b). Concatenated exploration: Notes on a neglected type of longitudinal reserch. *Quality & Quantity*, 26, 435-442.

Stebbins, R.A. (1993a). *Career, culture and social psychology in a variety art: The magician* (reprinted ed.). Malabar, FL: Krieger.

Stebbins, R.A. (1993b). *Predicaments: Moral difficulty in everyday life*. Lanham, MD: University Press of America.

Stebbins, R.A. (1993c). *Canadian football. A view from the helmet*. (reprinted ed.). Toronto, ON: Canadian Scholars Press.

Stebbins, R.A. (1994a). The liberal arts hobbies: A neglected subtype of serious leisure. *Loisir et Société/Society and Leisure*,16, 173-186.

Stebbins, R.A. (1994b). *The franco-calgarians: French language, leisure, and linguistic lifestyle in an anglophone city*. Toronto, ON: University of Toronto Press.

Stebbins, R.A. (1995). *The connoisseur's New Orleans*. Calgary, AB: University of Calgary Press.

Stebbins, R.A. (1996a). *The barbershop singer: Inside the social world of a musical hobby*. Toronto, ON: University of Toronto Press.

Stebbins, R.A. (1996b). Volunteering: A serious leisure perspective. *Nonprofit and Voluntary Action Quarterly*, 25, 211-224.

Stebbins, R.A. (1996c). Cultural tourism as serious leisure. *Annals of Tourism Research*, 23, 948-950.

Stebbins, R.A. (1996d). *Tolerable differences: Living with deviance* (2nd ed).. Toronto, ON: McGraw-Hill Ryerson.

Stebbins, R.A. (1996e). Casual and serious leisure and post-traditional thought in the information age. *World Leisure & Recreation*, 38 (3), 4-11.

Stebbins, R.A. (1997a). Casual leisure: A conceptual statement. *Leisure Studies*, 16, 17-25.

Stebbins, R.A. (1997b). Lifestyle as a generic concept in ethnographic research. *Quality & Quantity*, 31, 347-360.

Stebbins, R.A. (Ed.) (1997c). *World Leisure & Recreation* (special issue on volunteerism and the leisure perspective), 39 (3), 3-33.

Stebbins, R.A. (1997d). Exploratory research as an antidote to theoretical stagnation in leisure studies. *Loisir et Société/Society and Leisure*, 20, 421-434.

Stebbins, R.A. (1998a). *After work: The search for an optimal leisure lifestyle*. Calgary, AB: Detselig.

Stebbins, R.A. (1998b). Of time and serious leisure in the information age: The case of the Netherlands. *Vrijetijdstudies*, 16, 19-32.

Stebbins, R.A. (1998c). Serious leisure and wayward youth. Paper presented at the Youth at Risk Seminar of the Leisure Education Commission of the World Leisure & Recreation Association, Northeastern Mexico University, Monterrey, October.

Stebbins, R.A. (1998d). *The urban francophone volunteer: Searching for personal meaning and community growth in a linguistic minority*. Vol. 3, No. 2 (New Scholars-New Visions in Canadian Studies quarterly monographs series). Seattle, Wash.: University of Washington, Canadian Studies Centre, 1998.

Stebbins, R.A., & Parker, S.R. (1994). Work and leisure: The experience dimension. Paper presented at the Annual Meeting of the Canadian Sociology and Anthropology Association, June, Calgary.

Taylor, B. (1995). Amateurs, professionals, and the knowledge of archaeology. *British Journal of Sociology*, 46, 499-508.

Thompson, A.M., III, & Bono, B.A. (1993). Work without wages: The motivation of volunteer firefighters. *American Journal of Economics and Sociology*, 52, 323-343.

Thompson, M.C. (1997a). *Volunteer firefighters: Our silent heroes*. Unpublished doctoral dissertation, University of Calgary.

Thompson, M.C. (1997b). Employment-based volunteering: Leisure or not? *World Leisure & Recreation*, 39 (3), 30-33.

Thompson, S. (1992). "Mum's tennis day": The gendered definition of older women's leisure. *Loisir et Société/Society and Leisure*, 15, 271-289.

Titmuss, R. (1970). *The gift relationship*. London, Eng.: Allen & Unwin.

Tomlinson, A. (1993). Culture of commitment in leisure: Notes towards the understanding of a serious legacy. *World Leisure & Recreation*, 35 (1), 6-9.

Truzzi, M. (1972). The occult revival as popular culture. *The Sociological Quarterly*, 13, 16-36.

UNESCO. (1976). Recommendation on the development of adult education. Paris, France.

Unruh, D.R. (1979). Characteristics and types of participation in social worlds. *Symbolic Interaction*, 2, 115-130.

Unruh, D.R. (1980). The nature of social worlds. *Pacific Sociological Review*, 23, 271-296.

Urry, J. (1990). *The tourist gaze: Leisure and travel in contemporary societies*. London, Eng.: Sage.

Van Til, J. (1988). *Mapping the third sector: Voluntarism in a changing political economy*. New York, NY: The Foundation Center.

Veal, A.J. (1993). The concept of lifestyle: A review. *Leisure Studies*, 12, 233-252.

Veblen, T. (1953). *The theory of the leisure class*. New York, NY: New American LIbrary.

Walker, J.W., Kimmel, D.C., & Price, K.F. (1980-1981). Retirement style and retirement satisfaction: Retirees aren't all alike. *International Aging and Human Development*, 12, 267-281.

Weinblatt, N., & Navon, L. (1995). Flight from leisure: A neglected phenomenon in leisure studies. *Leisure Studies*, 17, 309-325.

Williamson, P. (1995). Occupation therapy and "serious" leisure: Promoting productive occupations through leisure. *Leisure-Options*, 5 (1), 61-64.

Wilson, K. (1995). Olympians or lemmings? The postmodernist fun run. *Leisure Studies*, 14, 174-185.

World Leisure and Recreation Association. (1994). WLRA international charter for leisure education. Sharbot Lake, ON.

World Tourism Organization (1985). *The role of recreation management in the development of active holidays and special interest tourism and consequent enrichment of the holiday experience*. Madrid, Spain: United Nations Development Program.

Wuthnow, R. (1991). *Acts of compassion: Caring for others and helping ourselves*. Princeton, N.J.: Princeton University Press.

Yair, G. (1990). The commitment to long-distance running and level of activities. *Journal of Leisure Research*, 22, 213-227.

Yair. G. (1992). What keeps them running? The "circle of commitment" of long distance runners. *Leisure Studies*, 11, 257-270.

Yankelovich, D. (1981). *New rules: Searching for self-fulfillment in a world turned upside down*. New York, NY: Random House.

Yiannakis, A., & Gibson, H. (1992). Roles tourists play. *Annals of Tourism Research*, 19, 287-303.

Yoder, D.G. (1997). A model for commodity intensive serious leisure. *Journal of Leisure Research*, 29, 407-429.

Zuzanek, J. (1996). Canada. In G. Cushman, A.J. Veal, & J. Zuzanek (Eds.), *World leisure participation: Free time in the global village* (pp. 35-76). Wallingford, Oxon, Eng.: CAB International

Index

191